Encounters
with a Fat
chemist

Encounters
with a Fat
chemist

Teaching at a University in Northern Cyprus

Chris Payne

authorHOUSE®

AuthorHouse™
1663 Liberty Drive
Bloomington, IN 47403
www.authorhouse.com
Phone: 1-800-839-8640

Published by AuthorHouse   05/22/2012

ISBN: 978-1-4685-7912-3 (sc)
ISBN: 978-1-4685-7913-0 (e)

Any people depicted in stock imagery provided by Thinkstock are models, and such images are being used for illustrative purposes only.
Certain stock imagery © Thinkstock.

This book is printed on acid-free paper.

Also by Chris Payne

Leaving the Eurozone—How a country can escape the tyrany of the Euro and go back to its own currency. (With Jeremy Cripps.) 2012

Contents

Preface

In the late flourishing of a humdrum career as a journeyman academic, I found myself, like some medieval artisan, moving from place to place and delivering classes, which, I hoped, would stimulate some resonance from my largely attentive and serious students. If I have any complaints about my students or my colleagues in the following memoir, then they are directed only at a small and unrepresentative minority. For the most part, in my long career, the pleasure of working with young active minds and the camaraderie of the common room have compensated, to a large degree, for the disappointments and setbacks of many battles against those endemic forces of reaction, parsimony and vindictiveness which are the signal features of all top-heavy, self-serving bureaucracies, nowhere more prominent than in university administration. There can be few greater pleasures in the life of an academic than to close the door of the classroom on one's problems and enjoy, for a limited period, a lively discourse with burgeoning young intelligences. That pleasure, and the creative freedom of a life of the mind, are the reasons one enters the academic priesthood in the first place.

So, my stopover in the Turkish Republic of Northern Cyprus, the TRNC, while full of difficulties, did, nonetheless, have its moments of satisfaction amidst our bemusement and frustration at the random illogicalities of the ways in which the American Institute of Cyrpus, and, indeed, the whole country, was run. It is best, we soon learned, that when living in a society whose national personality was surreal absurdity, to strive to retain one's sense of humour. As Federico Garcia Lorca famously put it, "For those who feel, life is a tragedy—for those who think it is a comedy." I pride myself that I am more of a thinker rather than a feeler and therefore I am at one with the great FGL. Living in the TRNC, in spite of the daily problems and difficulties, was definitely a comedy. It is in that spirit that this account of my year and a half living and working there has been written.

As in all walks of life, one meets the odd unhinged individual, and The Fat Chemist of the title was certainly one of those. And there were one or two people who tended to ludicrous puffed-up self-aggrandisement as would-be world players in the AIC, a university which is actually ranked lower than two-thousandth best of the all the universities of the world.

But for the most part, people were becomingly modest, not to say kind and friendly. Fellow academics in the Faculty of Economics and Business were mostly well-disposed towards us and I wish them all well. The names of all the people I got to know and like would be too long. But I thank particularly, Reban, Celusk and Turan from the Department of Management Information Systems who did a fine job of staying confident and cheerful in the worst of working conditions. And there were Rick and Dick, AIC panjandrums, who did important things, I know not what, in the Institute's high office up in the white shining Rectorate Building on top of the hill. My admiration also goes to Rector Nilgun Sarp who tried valiantly and admirably, but ultimately unsuccessfully, to impose proper academic standards and procedures on the place. I must especially single out Erkal, our regular taxi-driver, who is one of those immensely talented individuals who knows everyone and knows how to get anything done.

Without Erkal's regular help in demystifying the complex and unfamiliar, our life in Cyprus would have been so much more difficult. And a special mention to Adnam, Sancho Panza to Erkal's Don Quixote, whose driving turned every journey with him into an exhilarating rollercoaster adventure. A thank-you list would not be complete without including Albertin, the proprietor of the CafeDaD, which became our habitual watering-hole, a final stop on the regular weekly circuit of cybercafé-supermarket-cafe. His cafe, which he ran with his family, was a haven where the English expatriates would gather on Saturday afternoons to watch British Premier League football played in real time on a wall-sized TV and which was, for many of us, a touch of home. There were so many other friendly, warm, amusing, delightful people, faculty, students, staff, too many to list, who amply compensated for the privations of exile.

Finally, I must thank my dear beloved Loydz, who probably did more than could fairly be asked of a dutiful wife in the sharing of my experience. She has been able to relive it anew as she has diligently proof-read my efforts while simultaneously making sure that I have kept my nose to the writer's grindstone.

One

Late in life, at the dog-end of a career of coruscating mediocrity, I found myself catapulted into the lifestyle of someone forty years younger. I had become, like those hippie-trail flower-children of my youth, an academic gypsy. At an age when those more successful in my chosen career than myself could settle back into comfortable and dignified retirement to reflect on their academic titles and revered publications, I had become an itinerant jobbing university teacher just like some twenty-something novice lecturer with a freshly-minted PhD, setting out on a round of short-term contracts and visiting positions. After their peregrinations, they would write a textbook, get themselves a tenured teaching job and move sedately up the academic greasy pole to the dizzy heights of professor, dean, provost or even rector. By contrast, I was living my life backwards. After having done my time in a number of English colleges and taking a grateful early retirement, I was suddenly on the road like a scholastic neophyte, moving from country to country and job to job. I could have been running away from something. Myself, maybe? Or it might just have been restlessness born of a short attention span which makes me tire of a place after a short time. Anyway, whatever the reason for my constant relocations and whatever the flaws in my character which led to them, I eventually found myself in the Turkish Republic of Northern Cyprus at the augustly—and pretentiously named American Institute of Cyprus.

Travel, as Paul Theroux put it, contracts the mind. The opposite, of course, to conventional wisdom. It is impossible to expect modern-day foreign travel to provide the sort of eye-opening illuminations of different lifestyles and customs which some of the more privileged members of previous generations might have enjoyed. Even twenty years ago, foreign travel was a comparatively rare treat for the English, being mostly confined to package tours to the Costa Blackpool where convenience and familiarity were assured along with the sunshine and a beneficial exchange rate. How quaint it now seems, even at such a short separation of time, that package tours needed to be carefully managed by 'reps', there on hand to guard the intrepid travellers from the dangers lurking around all the corners of strange and dangerous places like Torremolinos and Benidorm, to say nothing of far-flung outposts of the likes of Corfu and Mykonos. Until very recently, non-packaged foreign travel had to be taken in bite-sized pieces—a day trip to buy decently-priced wine in Calais, for example. (Or Basildon-sur-Mer, as it could easily be known, given that so much of that part of northern France is devoted to catering for the British.) Or maybe a group of brave souls—safety in numbers—might take an overnight football trip to Milan or Barcelona.

I don't know if the English, universally famous for their insularity, still see 'abroad' that way anymore, my having spent so long on some foreign academic jaunt or another. Don't get me wrong when I say 'jaunt'. I worked hard at all my postings and I am sure I gave value for money as I delivered my classroom performances. It is just that I never stayed long in any one town or city before some new assignment drew me away. My teaching style, a declamatory high-energy delivery in received English came across, I am sure, as strangely exotic to the students. And, having unconsciously cultivated an accent not unlike that spoken by the Prince of Wales, I was something of a curiosity. But I never had any complaints and my many students were usually politely kind about my classes. Mostly they were genuinely complimentary about my efforts and sometimes they even terminated our shared experience with a touching small gift.

Apart from my Englishness, I also had the advantage of a marketable academic subject—computing and information systems. If I had been a historian or sociologist, say, I have no doubt that my limited talents would not have been in such demand. Even less employable, of course, are graduates with degrees in subjects like English literature, who are turned out in their thousands by the British production line. They can find jobs abroad if they are able to convert their skills into being able to teach English as a foreign language but, on its own, the ability to read Thomas Hardy in the original is not too impressive in a world where the emphasis in most places is skill in business, management, finance and IT, the 'in-demand' subjects of the 21st century. So, my background in mathematics, computing and information systems management was often exactly what was needed.

Most countries have a number of what are known as 'American' universities, backed by a sister institution in the United States, where the teaching is in English to an American curriculum. It was there, I found my customary niche. And in such places, I would often be the only 'Brit' on campus. I found this situation to be quite pleasant. There still remains a little relict prestige in being a Briton surrounded by Americans and, as a result, I made good friends in all the places I worked.

I like the democratic atmosphere of American colleges and universities. I like especially being able to talk on equal terms with senior university people, something which is very difficult to do in the UK. There is always a feeling in England that in any interpersonal encounter it is one's social class which is being weighed up, not the value of what one is saying. The idea that a humble lecturer could talk to a college principal on level terms is still regarded as absurd in parts of the British academic establishment. I can't remember exactly how many times I was ever permitted to speak directly to the principal of a British college, but it could certainly be counted on the fingers of both hands. In all my thirty years in the British system, I was never once invited to speak to a vice-chancellor except when he was presenting me with my degree. In England, there is never any of that sense of personal equality you get when you talk to senior Americans because Americans treat senior management more as a job than a social rank. And, what is more, they never could guess, as an Englishman instantly could, that I am from a lower social caste with its unspoken implication that I am therefore deficient in ambition and career expectations.

In spite of what a lot of British academics would have you believe, the scholastic standards in the US are generally much higher than those in the UK. I remember a British teacher of accountancy telling me how much better was her institution, a moderate polytechnic, than the University of Maryland in Baltimore, where I had just returned from a year as a visiting associate professor. I had to point out to her that it was a University of Maryland graduate who had won that year's Nobel Chemistry prize—something that her lowly institution would never achieve.

So with all this travel, how do I rate Theroux's observation? Well, my mind has certainly been narrowed by all this foreign travel. When I made my first trip across Europe in 1995 to go to work in Heidelberg, I remember stopping the car by the side of a country road one autumn morning just to take in the 'strangeness' of the place—the different shapes of the fields and the towns, the unusual smells, the layout of road junctions and telephone wires, the adverts for exotic drinks with unpronounceable names, the relative emptiness of the terrain. All those myriad small differences impinging simultaneously on one's consciousness—they spelt 'abroad' to a provincial Englishman.

Now, though, fifteen years down the track, little of such wonderment remains. Familiarity with foreign places may be one reason why places once synonymous with 'terra incognita—here be dragons'—like, maybe, Sofia or Thessaloniki, now hold no terrors and few surprises. A decade and a half of renting apartments, riding in taxis, arguing with students, getting paid, opening and closing bank accounts, going to the supermarket and sitting around in bars have left me with a feeling of the sameness of the human experience everywhere.

So they don't speak English and I don't speak Bulgarian? It doesn't matter. There is a universal language of signs, obligations, customs and expectations which work pretty well everywhere. Remember your manners, keep smiling, say 'please' and 'thank you', praise their football team, admire the children, pay your rent on time, give a ten per cent tip to waiters and taxi drivers. These, and a few other simple rules, will get you a long way. A simple international vocabulary is often all you need—'vino','pay now', 'taxi', 'Manchester United' *etc* . . . Add a few bits of sign language—tap the glass for another drink, do imaginary writing on left palm to get the bill—and you are well on the way to becoming a fully-fledged cosmopolitan. And every language has an all-purpose word to be used when you don't know what to say. In French it's 'd'accord', in Greek it's 'endaxi', in Turkish they say 'tammam' and the English cannot get by without 'cheers'. It is very important to learn this portmanteau word first.

The other mind-narrowing experience of foreign travel is the way that all countries, and certainly the big cities, are starting to look the same, probably because of the influence of Hollywood culture, mass tourism, the widespread use of English and the globalisation of the construction and automobile industries. There can be few capital cities which do not have a Holiday Inn where you can watch CNN in your world-standard room and where the taxis are yellow or cream-coloured Mercedes. The big cities with their skyscrapers, underpasses and pedestrian walkways are, architecturally-speaking, virtually indistinguishable, save for the small 'old town' or Roman ruin, kept tidy but undeveloped for the tourists. If I ever get to visit Valparaiso, say, or Ulan Bator, I am sure I will be able to find my way around it using a street map of Dortmund. My own private theory is all human settlements aspire to the condition of Croydon. The world is getting smaller and is evening out into a bland homogeneity. There can no longer be any village or remote hamlet anywhere in the world which will not shortly be able to boast its own Starbucks or Kentucky Fried Chicken.

Even the banknotes in different countries are similar, designed and printed, as they mostly are, to a standard pattern by Messrs De La Rue. For example, the British blue twenty pound note resembles the twenty euro note save for the superficialities of design details such as the image of Queen Elizabeth. It also resembles, in size and colour, the Bulgarian 20 lev, the Turkish 20 lira and the Philippines 100 peso notes. What is more, they are all good for buying dinner for one in their respective countries, regardless of the advertised foreign exchange rates. Lunch, of course, is usually half the price of dinner and therefore costs a red one. The little green ones are good for a taxi ride.

My mind has been narrowed by travel in another, more personal way. Before I travelled to foreign climes, I had adopted the more-or-less obligatory belief set of the liberal educated Englishman. The required position was an arrogant, left-of-centre, patronising, colonial guilt about the non-British and their manifest misfortune at having lost out on the first place in the lottery of life. Not to take on this position would soon find oneself ostracised in the staff rooms of British universities and colleges where only acceptable political position is held by someone who has been force-fed on *Guardian* editorials. A few years on the road and I soon adjusted—most people abroad neither know much about the UK, nor do they care. What a waste of all that mind-numbing moral navel-gazing!

My travels made me see that people are very much the same everywhere, with pretty much the same attitudes and ambitions. Cultural differences are relatively superficial compared with common humanity. I no longer had to size them up to try to work out what attitude it would be correct to assume when communicating with them. Those liberal attitudes were gone forever now that I had managed to rid my mind of a lot of redundant intellectual baggage. Even better, the brain-space which had been freed up by my cast-off ideas was not filled up by any replacement mental polystyrene. I simply stopped having 'beliefs', or at least not so many. The relief of discarding long-worn-out attitudes was not unlike the feeling one gets from unloading a heavy burden one has carried for too long.

I like being an expatriate for another reason that could be considered mind-narrowing. The great thing about being abroad is that you neither know nor care about the internal politics and injustices of your host country. You are there as a guest and you must disport yourself accordingly but as for involvement in civic or national or political affairs, you have no responsibility at all. Nor would you be welcomed if you had the impertinence to take an interest. This is a glorious liberation. When I am home in England, I am continually offended by the ignorance and criminality of British politicians and business leaders and the rancid smell of entrenched, institutional greed which pervades all British public life. As a result, I regularly find myself in blood pressure danger for getting angry at the dim-witted vindictiveness and transparent selfishness of those people in charge of the running British domestic institutions like the health service and the universities. After just a few weeks back in my home country, I find myself seething with rage and contempt.

This is because I feel, oddly, that I have an obligation to, somehow, be involved in the British system, if only to write letters and to make my views felt. I feel, possibly wrongly, that it is part of my duty as a tax-paying citizen of a democratic country that that is what I should do. But one feels none of that in a foreign country where you can't read the newspapers or understand the TV and your only obligation to the host state is not to involve yourself with it because its workings are none of your business.

So with my mind nicely narrowed already after ten years on the road, it just remained for Northern Cyprus, the 'Jewel of the Mediterranean', to finish the job and compress it even further. Which it duly did.

The island of Cyprus nestles in the far eastern armpit of the Mediterranean. Over the centuries, armies and politicians have exploited its strategic location on the fault line between Christian and Muslim. The fault line has not faded in recent times. Far from it. There is a fairly impenetrable so-called 'Green Line' which divides the ethnically homogeneous Levantine population of the island between Muslim, Turkish-speaking north, known as the 'Turkish Republic of Northern Cyprus' or TRNC from the Greek-speaking Orthodox Christian south, known simply as the 'Republic of Cyprus'. Physiognomically and culturally the two communities are, to an outsider, completely indistinguishable save for their languages and religions. But after five hundred years of the inevitable genetic intermixing which must have taken place between the two communities when they were stilll unsegregated, the two groups still cling to positions inherited from the fifteenth century—mutual hatred, suspicion and fear. Repeated efforts by British colonisers and international agencies to bang the Turkish and Greek heads together to try to provoke a realisation of their common entangled genetic legacy have always foundered on the rocks of those five centuries of reciprocal loathing.

On the surface, Cyprus remains an edenic fable. For three hundred days a year the sun shines on a breath-taking landscape, Exotic fruits grow in every garden and on every scrap of spare land—olives, lemons and figs, even nectarines and melons are there for the picking. The clean, clear surrounding sea yields a generous harvest of fish for those delicious *al fresco* Cypriot lunches at charming harbour-side restaurants. On hot summer evenings the heavy scents of jasmine and bougainvillea fill the air with the defining fragrances of exoticism and sensuality.

Being where it is, or maybe because of its sheer desirability as a place to live, Cyprus has a complex and violent history of being fought over by innumerable armies and peoples, each of which has left its mark before being supplanted by a usurper. The result is a palimpsest of multiple archeological strata whose many visible remains add a further element of beauty and fascination to the rich natural backdrop. The ruins of the ancient buildings of bronze age peoples, of ancient Greeks and Romans, of Venetians and many other long-gone temporary occupants mix with the oleander blossoms and the lush foliage amid which are hidden small restaurants serving delicious Mediterranean meals of recently-caught fish, warm bread, fruit fresh off the tree and local dark red wine. There has been little by the way of town planning—Cypriot towns and cities have Greek columns cheek by jowl with Romanesque arches. Medieval Crusader cathedrals have been converted to mosques by the simple expediency of bolting on a couple of minarets. These days the natural charm is added to by low-level, three and four storey apartment blocks with none of those skyscrapers which have despoiled so much of the Mediterranean littoral. The Cypriots have sensibly resisted the temptation to permit the construction of profitable high-rise residential blocks in tourist areas.

With the result that coastal resorts still have the charm of small towns. As the cream-painted low-level apartment blocks age and the palm trees grow between them, they fit snugly and naturally into the townscape.

Naturally, such an enchanted garden is a magnet to those looking for a relaxed lotus-eating life, especially those retirees from the European north. There is a large semi-permanent population of older people retiring from the grey cold of Manchester, Mönchengladbach or Minsk, a population large enough that the Northern Cyrpus government has recently attempted to staunch the flow of incomers by the introduction of stringent rules to control immigration. Residency qualifications have been gradually extended over the years and now stand at a fifteen year waiting period. South of the Green Line though, runs the writ of the European Union and residency qualification for EU citizens is easier, although, as a result, house prices and other living costs there are considerably higher.

The Green Line buffer zone is administered by UN diplomats and since partition in 1974 there has been a permanent presence of UN troops with their distinctive sky-blue berets. Movement between the two sides is carefully controlled by each side's local immigration police. On moving from the Turkish to the Greek side in Nicosia, which the Turks call 'Lefkosa', one must present one's residency documents first to the Turkish police and then to their Greek counterparts. Between the two frontier posts, there is 500 metres of road lined with derelict houses, unoccupied since the war of 1974. Here and there UN soldiers stand around or sit in their Land Rovers but for the most part they leave the policing of the frontier to the local people, relying on the bitter determination of each side to prevent any member of the wrong group getting through.

We had little difficulty passing through these checkpoints. Naturally, my wife, Loydz, being Filipina, was questioned as if she were a security risk but we soon came to understand the attitudes of the gate-keepers.

Britons like myself with European passports could come and go as they please and thus their wives would be let through after a just little token questioning. No, the main, the only, aim of the border guards was to keep out the wrong type of Cypriot.

In a multinational community such as Cyprus, the various national groups tend to stay in their own enclaves. According to our taxi-driver, who knew absolutely everything one needed to know about Kyrenia, as well as everybody, the Germans had formed an identifiable group until a few years ago and had then starting selling up their apartments and going home. Consequently, we met very few Germans while we lived there.

However, there were still many Russians, some of whom were reputed not to be able to go back to Mother Russia for various reasons best left unmentioned. We heard little Russian in the main streets of Kyrenia, the main town of the area-the Russian people tended to stay in a number of russianised new housing developments a few miles up the coast. But there were several Russian students in my evening classes who were long-term residents.

By far the biggest group of Kyrenian residents were the ethnic Turkish from the mainland. Houses and apartment blocks were springing up continuously, many to be occupied immediately on completion by newly-arrived Turkish colonists. Fifty years ago, Kyrenia had been a cosmopolitan Greek city. Now all traces of Greek influence had been extirpated. The only local language to be heard and seen was Turkish.

As everywhere, the expatriate British are unmissable. In every restaurant or bar one could pick out the accents of Leeds or Peckham or Birmingham. The accents would usually be owned by a couple of pensioners who had cashed in some of the inflated value of their house in the UK to buy a flat or small house in Northern Cyprus where prices were at a level not seen in the UK these last twenty years. These couples, pallid English complexions scorched scarlet by the cruel Cyprus sun, could be seen and heard drifting around the town from bar to bar, exchanging day-old copies of *The Daily Mail* and discussing the relative merits of Manchester United and Aston Villa. The bars themselves would often also be owned by British expatriates who would always be sure to include fish and chips and the all-day full English breakfast as menu staples.

Another feature of the British presence was the existence of a British Residents Society, a version of which automatically springs into life whenever two or three Brits are gathered together in some foreign country. These societies are ostensibly mutual-help groups for expatriate Britons adrift in an alien environment. They organise small get-togethers such as wine and cheese parties, they collect paperback books for resale for charity and they provide a source of useful information for the UK citizen lost abroad. How useful they are in today's standardised, converged world is difficult to judge. But the British Residents Society does have a latent importance. It provides an outlet for the considerable energies of those active retired busybody Englishwomen who find themselves at a loose end after a lifetime of organising husband, children and jobs.

To the resident British contingent should be added those semi-residents who would go home for extended periods. Amazingly, they would often depart between November and March when the British weather is at its bleakest. At first, it was difficult to understand this pattern of behaviour until we had to spend a winter in Cyprus ourselves. Then all became clear: the British go home for Christmas, not out of religious duty or family obligation but for the simple reason that Cypriot homes, built to cool its occupants from the fierce summer heat, do not have central heating, double glazing or insulation. We did ask our taxi driver why houses were not winter-proofed in any way. He shook his head as if not understanding my question.

"Cyprus always ver' cold in winter."

In other words the local people simply put up with the winter discomfort and await the return of spring.

Another identifiable British sub-group is the house-hunters. These tended to be sociologically indistinguishable from the long-term residents i.e. pensioner couples often scouting out retirement homes on the island. The house-hunters would usually appear in great numbers in the cooler spring or autumn months during school term-time when many special deals were available on the only recently-instituted direct flights. Flights in and out of the TRNC were an international problem since Turkish Northern Cyprus is a country which is only recognised by Turkey and Syria. This means that all flights to and from the TRNC would need to land in Turkey on their way in or out of the country. Until 2006, passengers would have needed to alight at a Turkish airport and endure endless problems involving visas and immigration. The new arrangement was that planes would now only need to touch down on Turkish soil for a token stopover while the passengers stayed aboard it. This new way of doing things would make it much easier to travel to the TRNC. Or would have, if the prices on the semi-direct flights had not been set at Concorde levels, a regular source of complaint from the British residents in general.

Newly-arrived British visitors, still pale from England and looking for a retirement address could sometimes be seen in the company of touts from the myriad local estate agencies, intent on separating the newcomers from their house equity or retirement payoff PDQ.

Housing and its prices occupies a central place in the psychology of the suburban Englishman or Englishwoman, easily taking up more mental energy than religion, or sex or even football. Housing in Turkophone Cyprus for British incomers was usually sold or rented by English estate agents, negotiated in English and priced in pounds sterling. Most of the agents would deal exclusively only with the British-the very large number of Turkish colonists had their own agencies back home in Turkey. To the British, house prices were set temptingly low in Kyrenia and the other coastal towns. In 2008, even before the world housing crash, it was possible to pick up a small apartment with use of a communal pool for as little as £30,000, a sum which used to amount only to about a year's price inflation of a medium-sized English suburban semi-detached in the Home Counties.

Many visitors were seduced by these apparent bargains. Imagine, many no doubt thought to themselves, a holiday home in the island paradise for less than the increase in the value of our semi in Sutton Coldfield or Guildford! Too good to be true? Well, yes, it cetainly was for many caught in this particular honey trap even before the bottom dropped out of the world housing market.

Buying a property in Turkish North Cyprus is not a bit like buying in Britain. For a start, these great deals which are advertised in every one of hundreds of estate agents are not for a finished dwelling. They are the price 'off-plan' i.e. the purchaser pays the developer in instalments while the house is being built and in doing so they provide the builder with a stream of working capital. The full amount due for the completed house or apartment may be spread over two or three years before the purchaser can take possession of what he has paid for.

The dangers of getting into this sort of deal ought to be obvious to anyone, especially the old and supposedly wise. What is to stop builder/developer just taking the money and scarpering? Well, yes, that is an ever-present risk and happens frequently as developers go bust, probably deliberately, mid-way through a development, after having spent all the cash provided by naïve British buyers. Then there was the popular scam of mortgaging off the land to raise extra capital in mid-development. Even if the house is actually built and handed over, the new occupants will not be able to resell it because they will not have a title to the land it is built on. Very occasionally, a British 'developer' working these scams would be caught and prosecuted in the UK, including one gentleman with the deliciously appropriate name of 'Mr Robb'.

In some cases the title, even if it did exist, will be useless in the long term because it may not even have been owned by the developer but may really have belonged to a displaced Greek now living in southern Cyprus who wants his land back and has the original title to prove he owns it. When the island was partitioned in 1974, very many similar displaced persons were created. To be fair, there are also many Turkish Cypriots who were long-time residents of the south and who are equally determined to reclaim their family property. The vast number of such cases, each one fraught with resentment and hunger for reparation is just one reason why attempts at reunification of north and south and reconciliation between Greek and Turk rarely get very far. There was a glimmer of hope for a settlement in 2004 when the then United Nations Secretary-General Kofi Annan came near to a resolution of the problem which sparked a frantic speculative housing boom. But the agreement soon foundered and the two communities settled back into their traditional mutual hatred, leaving a landscape littered with half-finished houses.

One might think that a former British colony would retain some of the legal framework which the British Empire exported to them which is generally acknowledged as one of Britain's major imperial achievements, along with red pillar boxes, driving on the left and the English language. Under a British legal code, property buyers would get some protection from this sort of criminality. Indeed, there does exist a code of law inherited from colonial times which, in theory at least, should ensure fair and just dealings between parties to a major transaction. But it does not work the way the law works in England. To start with, any lawyer you deal with will almost certainly be a cousin or brother or in-law or friend of the developer, a relationship which will, let us say, militate against his natural lawyerly inclinations to be even-handed. And second, if you are not a Turkish Cypriot or even Turkish, you may well find that your case somehow never gets to the top of the lawyer's in-tray.

A third reason why you are out on your own when buying property in the TRNC is that it is not recognised as a country by almost any other state than Turkey, except possibly Syria. This means that there is no extradition or deportation for those who live there, either native or foreign-born. As a result, it is a country without restraints on how it runs its internal affairs. Thus many international criminals find it a congenial place from which to work their illicit business. Your small-time dishonest property developer is no more than a small cog in a large network of criminals and semi-criminals on the make. His primary reference will not be to his customer, but to the lawyer, or for that matter to the local and national politicians, to other dubious businessmen, all the way up to the major figures at the top—senior politicians, expatriate money-launderers, tax-evaders, East European mafiosi and drug dealers—the people who actually own and run the country, foreign customers, especially British infidels, do not rate highly on his list of obligations.

On the other hand, everyday life in this gangsterocracy is fairly safe. There is little petty crime or street violence. The senior *capos* do not want the sort of atmosphere which is likely to scare away the punters. The small-time rascal—the pickpocket or street thug-who would find a niche market in a larger and thus less connected criminal fraternity such as exists in London, would have no opportunities for freelancing in the TRNC outside of the close-knit family network and the strong criminal management structure.

So what brought me and my new wife to the Turkish Republic of Northern Cyprus for a flirtation with hell? Hell—what about the sunshine and the scenery, the fascinating history and the exotic expatriate lifestyle in what most people would regard as a very desirable place to live indeed?

It is a question I have asked myself many times. I had a very good job as a professor of mathematics in a well-known American university based in Germany when I first saw an advert for faculty to work in Kyrenia while I was perusing the Chronicle of Higher Education, the recognised market place for the hiring of international university teachers.

I was about to collect my bus pass which for non-British readers, I should explain, is English slang for approaching the usual retirement age of 65, when one becomes officially old and is awarded for longevity with an old-age state pension and free travel on British buses. I had only a few working years left and I could see that my job with the American university in Germany would soon be coming to an end anyway. I was sorry because it had been a big part of my life for getting on for twenty years and I was used to it. But the US Army and the US Air Force, who supplied contractually all of our students, were undergoing radical change. The military bases in NATO countries, where most of classes were held, were closing down as the military personnel in them were re-deployed. From being temporary members of a standing garrison in Germany, the UK, Italy etc. where American servicemen and their families had lived a quiet life for three generations, our students suddenly found themselves in action in Iraq and Afghanistan. The university, headquartered in Washington DC, but with a very successful division in Europe, had therefore begun a programme of cutbacks of senior faculty members and I watched my senior colleagues gradually being made redundant. Some went back home to USA. Others were offered postings in the new war zones in Iraq or Afghanistan or other hostile places. Being a near-pensioner and well over the age for bivouacing in a tent in a war-zone, and, what is more, now having a new wife, I felt this might be the time to take a chance on Cyprus. This would be something new and different after the comfortable life I had enjoyed in Heidelberg-which is surely one of Europe's most stylish and beautiful cities, for which reason it had been sensibly chosen in 1945 as the headquarters of the United States Army in Europe.

It was summer of 2006 and Loydz and I had married the previous April. We had begun our married life living in my bachelor apartment overlooking the Neckar River. By this time I was already looking at other jobs and Loydz' feeling of alienation prompted me to do something about it. It had not been easy for an Englishman to break into what is essentially a closed expatriate group like the American academic community in Germany. Most of us in that group had worked and played together for years and we had established life-long friendships. The work of the university took place right across the NATO area and its teachers and professors were used to living an exciting itinerant lifestyle which involved spending a month or two at a different European garrison town before moving on. This mobile working life generated a very strong cameraderie among the faculty. I can see why my wife felt a sense of exclusion, especially since she also had no words of German.

So I handed in my notice at Heidelberg and wrote to accept the offer from the American Institute of Cyprus. I was going to be Head of Department of Management Information Systems with the rank of full professor. Moving day would be August 31st 2007, still ten weeks away. We began plans for the move including packing up all our belongings in Heidelberg and taking them to storage at my house in France. After several years on the road for the university, I had first gone to live full-time in Heidelberg three years before with a car-load of stuff. It took several journeys with a Ford Transit van to move it all back, so much it had grown. I sometimes wonder if one's objects and possessions are not mere inanimate things: I have a theory that they breed among themselves when we humans are not watching.

But never fast enough to fill up the French house which I had bought several years previously for one of my previous failed attempts at retirement. It was a large Breton *longère* which could hold anything we could stuff into it. Packing up my life in Heidleberg was a sadness but life is a journey and one must move on. So on the last Friday evening of my job there we got into a hired car with two or three suitcases and said our final goodbyes, my head still throbbing from hangover from the lavish going-away party my colleagues had generously hosted for us the night before. Just over an hour later, after the drive up the autobahn to Frankfurt airport, a drive which had so frightened me when I had first arrived in Germany some eleven years previously, we were checking into an airport hotel in preparation for an early flight to Istanbul the following morning.

Two

That was where the plan came unstuck. We had been in extensive correspondence with the Human Resources Department of the AIC in Kyrenia during the run-up to our planned move and we had assumed that they were as competent and knowledgeable as similar departments in all the other universities I have worked for. We had emailed and telephoned repeatedly to confirm that Loydz would not need a visa to travel to Northern Cyprus. This was a concern based on our long experience of arguments with immigration police, who look on a Philippine passport the way an ayatollah might regard a practical handbook of militant feminism. To an immigration official, being Filipina is a deeply seditious admission that the owner is a threat to all civilised western values. Hence the requests for repeated assurances that there would be no problems. None at all, HR regularly confirmed, the Turkish Republic of Northern Cyprus is a visa-free zone. A lifetime of being let down by people who have told me 'trust me' or 'don't worry' should have warned me and when we approached the check-in next morning, I was proved right. The clerk dutifully labelled our suitcases and processed our tickets, both my free ticket and the one I had just bought for Loydz. At the last minute she decided to take a closer look at the innumerable stamps in Loydz' alien travel document. After about three minutes of flicking through the pages she picked up the phone and phoned the duty immigration policeman.

"Nein?"

"Nein!"

She turned to us.

"Sie haben kein Visa!! This is very bad! I cannot let you board the plane! You must get a visa from the Turkish Embassy in your home country!"

Which is just a little Catch-22, given that to go back to Manila to get a visa for entry to Turkey requires that one changes planes in Istanbul, for which one needs a visa for Turkey.

Our mistress of German officiousness then turned around and threw our cases off the belt. We could do nothing except put them on a trolley and decide what to do next. My feelings then about The American Institute of Cyrpus remain unprintable to this day. On their assurances, I had given up a good job, I had spent prodigiously on sending our belongings to Kyrenia, on vehicle hire, on hotels and shipping charges. In return for which we now found ourselves publicly embarrassed and left sitting in the Frankfurt airport coffee shop at 7.00am, wondering what to do next.

What we did do was to rent another car and drive to the house in France. I might have no job, but at least we would have a roof over our heads. As for an income, we could survive on my pensions and our savings. So we set off on the 1000 km drive from Frankfurt to Brittany and, after stopping over Saturday night south of Paris, we arrived at the house on Sunday afternoon just in time to enjoy an electrical blackout, thoughtfully laid on for our welcome by Electricité de France.

The following year was unexpectedly satisfying. We cleaned the place, installed new bathrooms and WC's and purchased some traditional Breton furniture including a wonderful *salle à manger bretonne,* a huge dining table with chairs and matching sideboard, all elaborately hand-carved in heavy oak.

During the first few months in France we made strenuous efforts to get some cooperation from the AIC in Kyrenia to send back a large box of personal effects, including our wedding photographs which we had sent on ahead and which were languishing somewhere in some stock room. After dozens of emails and phone calls, we managed to pin down the box as being somewhere in the Faculty of Business and Economics. Eventually, I managed to get to speak to the Faculty Secretary, Cemaliye.

"I am very sorry to bother you, but you have my box. Could you please, please put it somewhere safe?"

"This is not part of my job!"

"I understand that but I am calling from western France and I can't get there to do it myself. All I want is that it is kept somewhere safe until I can work out what to do to get it back."

"This is not my job but I will do you a favour, just this one time."

"Thank you Cemaliye, thank you very much!"

"Remember, I am only doing this as a favour. It is not part of my job!!"

"I understand, Cemaliye, thank you very, very much indeed!"

Another round of emails and phone calls ascertained that the Institute would be willing to send the box back and yet a few more messages got me an estimate from DHL for bringing it to France. Loydz had meanwhile taken a couple of months leave back in Manila to greet her new grandson and to avoid the worst of a western European winter. So instead of risking having the box sent via DHL, I decided to go to Cyprus to collect it myself for about same cost as the postage.

Holding the famous burgundy European passport means that one can travel almost anywhere without the need to get a visa ahead of time. Thus my flight from Paris to Ercan, North Cyprus's only international airport, was uneventful. I arrived in Ercan late in the evening and took a taxi to a hotel in Kyrenia. I offered the driver a choice of euros or pounds sterling for the fare. He waved his hand airily.

"Money is money" he told me.

What an appropriate national motto, I thought. How much more does 'money is money' reflect the Turkish Republic of Northern Cyprus than some pompous high-minded platitude like 'E Pluribus Unum' or 'Liberté, Egalité, Fraternité'. Maybe other countries could follow suit and adopt national slogans closer to their national characters instead of posting sententious mission statements in dead languages. For example, Germany could use 'Alles in Ordnung' and Australia something like 'Surf, Beer and Meat Pies.'

When I arrived at the American Institute of Cyrpus, I was first stunned by its location on the gentle slopes between the clear blue Mediterranean and the dramatic vertical sweep of the Kyrenian mountains. I was given the red-carpet treatment by the welcoming senior staff. It was made clear to me that if I still wanted the job, I could still have it starting the beginning of the Fall semester. I was bought lunch and introduced to the Rector, whom I thought a kindly civilised man. I also met a variety of international and Turkish faculty who all assured me of the infinite desirability of being a faculty member in Kyrenia. Only the then Head of MIS, who was departing and whose job I was being courted for, sounded a cautionary note.

"Let's take a walk."

He steered me around the back of the Institute's buildings where we would not be overheard by the gushing welcoming committee.

"No," he went on, "this is a strange place. I am anxious to leave. I need to get back to Canada. The problem here is the old families. If you are not connected, your life will be very difficult."

Now when someone says things like that, it could either be well-meant advice or it could just be sour grapes grown from bitter soil. I stayed non-committal.

"But," he told me, "you have all the right qualifications for this job. They always have problems getting MIS faculty."

Shortly after I got back to France and after a long discussion with Loydz, we decided that, should I be re-offered the head's job, I would take it and then when I was duly offered it, I accepted.

We then completed the remaining house restoration tasks over the next six months, selected our best furntiture and household objects for storage and contacted several estate agents in Brittany in what we both felt would be a hopeless quest to sell the house. This time Loydz had remembered, when she had been in Manila, to get a full set of passport rubber stamps enough to satisfy even the most nit-picking of immigration officials.

This time was not just about work. We were able to visit England a couple of times to buy tropical clothes, to socialise with my family on the occasion of my 65th birthday and to attend a very enjoyable picture-framing course—an activity which I had earmarked for myself if I were ever able to retire.

I was also diagnosed with some permanent eye problems and changed my appearance when I was forced to discard my contact lenses in favour of regular eyeglasses. On the last day in France for a year we even managed to sell our old car, which had started first time when he had arrived a year previously from Germany but which, after a year's blameless service, had now earned a good home. Saying goodbye to our car, whom we had chistened Pierre, felt like pensioning off a hard-working domestic servant.

But with all medical, logistical, official and financial odds and ends carefully tied off and, we hoped, all possible angles covered, we boarded to TGV to Paris Charles de Gaulle airport and the flight to Cyprus for, who could tell, a new life in the sun.

Three

After all the problems the previous year, we finally made it to North Cyprus via London and Istanbul. A Friday afternoon taxi from Plésidy to Dinard then an evening flight to London Stansted, a night in a hotel in London, then the Saturday afternoon flight to Istanbul which arrived at midnight followed by a five-hour overnight wait on the iron benches of Istanbul Airport for the early morning hop to Ercan in Cyprus.

After travelling for the best part of two days we were exhausted. But Tugce, a very obliging and welcoming student, was waiting with the bus to the Institute.

"Wait please. Just a little longer. Maybe an hour, maybe two, who knows? Some other faculty are coming."

"We're sorry but we just can't wait. We are so tired. We have to sleep now."

So we took a taxi to the Institute's dormitory where free accommodation was laid on and we tumbled into bed to sleep away Sunday.

It was still mid-September and the Cyprus heat was still at its worst. This was something of a shock even for Loydz who comes from a tropical country—albeit one where temperatures are never much higher than 30C. I have been to the Philippines many times—the temperatures there are always comfortable—unlike Cyprus where the summer heat can be health-threatening.

Monday, we took the free shuttle bus to the Institute to begin the final stage of my long academic career as, I thought, Head of the Department of Management Information Systems.

After being told of the arrangements for paying salary and the total absence of medical, pension or social benefits, I was shown to my desk. Not office, note, but a 'desk'. Already occupying half the room was Reban, a man who was making a return to the land of his birth after many years toiling in the lower echelons of the English chalkface at a grim community college on the grey outreaches of the Essex marches. Reban was to be an Assistant Professor of MIS and we were to share, it turned out, the smallest office I have ever been assigned, even as a student. The storage space was limited to three cupboards between the two of us and the desk I had been assigned was dangerously wonky, with a heavy glass top given to sliding dangerously if something heavy were placed on it.

Reban was, he told me, sick of the English climate, the arbitrary bureaucracy of the British educational regulatory system and the pompous self-importance of community college commissars.

"It may well be the same here," I told him, "in my experience education bureaucrats are pretty much the same the world over."

"Oh yes, of course they are," he said," but here there is the sunshine, the mountains. Just look at that scenery!"

As we were debating the benefits and drawbacks of the expatriate teacher's lifestyle, the door of our tiny office was flung open and in strode a large Turkish woman with a grim expression. This was my first meeting with The Fat Chemist or TFC, as we soon started to call her. She was a fat middle-aged woman with a distinct body odour and the sort of face that I have seen before on people I have learned on bitter experience to dislike intensely. It is the face of anger, self-pity and resentful inner disappointment. The folds in her face had settled into a downswept curve of unsmiling contempt and the bottle-bottom glasses magnified the popping eyes of hyperthyroidism. Her arrogance and self-importance only served to underline her florid ugliness. In the end, we are, each of us, responsible for our own face.

She was, I realised there and then, going to be a problem and the sort of problem which would bring me face to face with an entirely unfamiliar culture of interpersonal relationships. There is a way of doing things which we use in most of the world i.e. you make a deal or a promise or a contract and then you keep it. There exists a basic quid pro quo—you treat me fairly and I will do the same for you. Bargains are made and kept and it works both ways.

But this simple give and take morality is regarded by the average Turkish Cypriot as incomprehensible naivety. What you should do, they understand, is to be a bit more street-wise. You enter into a deal with someone and wait until they have committed to their half of the bargain. Then you take the money and run!!

Of course this is not honest to anyone but a Cypriot and even he would never treat his brother or his friend that way. But the Cypriots, with personalities formed through generations of self-pitying mistrust of all things foreign and certainly all things western, do not consider non-Cypriots to be completely deserving of what we English would consider honest treatment. Time after time, non-Cypriot students would bring me stories about being cheated by the locals, often even by the Institute itself-which would cheerfully overcharge its own faculty and students for whatever it could get away with it.

When I had taken the job it had been on the understanding that I would be the head of the MIS Department. After all, that was what was in my contract. Two days before we had left France, I had looked up my name on the AIC website and sure enough, there I was listed as Head of Department. A day later, I looked again and although my name appeared ahead of the other members of the department, someone had removed my new title. But I thought nothing of it, reasoning that since the website was being changed on a daily basis, the omission was no more than an oversight.

That I should be the head of department could not be doubted. I was the only full professor and I had been teaching all the subjects of the Institute's undergraduate and graduate MIS curricula for many years. But I had not factored in the malice and deviousness of The Fat Chemist.

"I am Assistant Professor Doctor of Management Information Systems and the Dean has made me Head of Department of Management Information Systems!!" she declared with a flourish.

The Dean had been a sudden appointment, a retread politician temporarily out of office. But he knew where his Turkish duty lay. As soon as the English professor was on the plane, he could be safely replaced by TFC. Does it matter that a department of information systems be under the charge of a chemist with absolutely no qualifications in anything to do with IT, except maybe the odd weekend course? In a western university, TFC would never get through the door, but this, as I was repeatedly told, is Cyprus. She wanted the job, she was very well-connected so she got the job, whether she knew how to do it or not.

She launched into a prepared speech.

"I have a PhD from Middle Eastern University and a second PhD from this university in Education," she began, clearly telling me that her two PhD's would trump my own single doctorate.

Actually, she was being less than fulsome with the truth: she had failed to mention that her first doctorate was not recognised outside Cyprus and no-one had ever seen her diploma. What is more, her doctorate in education was still in progress. These facts were courtesy of Hussein, a very civilised man back in Cyprus after teaching at London University, who subsequently joined the disappeared ones when, for no discernible reason, his face one day stopped fitting. There were mutterings that his dismissal had been 'political'. I soon learnt that such disappearances were commonplace.

TFC continued to sing her own praises.

"My PhD thesis was in polymer chemistry and I wrote the best paper of my year. It was cited by many other chemists!"

As if that were not enough to put me in my place, she next tried to make it clear that she was even more well-travelled than I am.

"I have been to Turkey many times as well as Germany and Slovenia where I went to a conference. And I have travelled to Syria and Lebanon."

I made non-committal noises and let her ramble on.

"That is why the Dean has made me Head of Department. Because I have the right experience."

So, I told myself, let us not be petty by resorting to a public argument with her right now. This was her turf and she held the temporary advantage. No point in showing my hand right off—better to hold one's fire for the right moment. She would soon, as I was eventually proved correct, unravel. After all, I could easily get on a plane and leave them to it. I had been recruited for the real and relevant background and experience which she did not have-so it would only be a matter of time before she was exposed as a phoney. Besides, she was obviously politically powerful, as she went on to explain in her continuing peroration.

"Yes, the Dean has made me Head of Department because he thinks I am the best person for the job. My cousin is the Prime Minister."

"We will make a very good team!" she exclaimed.

"You, Assistant Professor Doctor Reban, will teach two courses of programming languages and two courses of web design and a course of operating systems. You Professor Doctor Christopher Payne, will teach three graduate courses in information systems and an undergraduate course in statistics."

Reban cut in.

"But I am a specialist in database. No-one is down to teach that course. I am no expert on operating systems but I could do the database course standing on my head."

"I am sorry!" she retorted angrily," but Fatih will be teaching database. He taught it last year and he is very good! He was my student! He is part-time."

This is the first time I had come across teaching time-tables being built around a part-timer's convenience since I taught at a grubby down-market technical college in the 1970's where the Principal's wife got first choice of part-time classes. (An interesting story. The principal was a drunk and lecher who preyed on the junior women teachers. His wife eventually got done for shop-lifting. But I digress.)

I joined the debate with Reban and TFC.

"Why are you asking me to teach statistics? There is a shortage of expertise in mainstream MIS in this department. There aren't enough MIS teachers to cover all the classes as it is. The place is awash with statistics teachers."

It was pointless.

"Professor Doctor Payne," she began haughtily, "I have read your CV. You have qualifications in mathematics and you will teach statistics! I had enough trouble with your predecessor over this."

By now she was shouting, her face scarlet with anger. I think she was recalling some imagined slight when my distinguished predecessor, an accomplished and well-known engineer, had also responded to her preremptory demands with insubordination and resentment. I was now starting to appreciate how prescient he had been with his warnings the previous March.

This, of course, is not the way it is done in a well-run university. Decisions are only made after due consultation—there is a fundamental respect for academic freedom which governs all discourse in university departments. Nothing could be more invidious than to give a fellow academic, especially a senior professor, a direct order concerning an academic matter. It offends against all principles of civilised scholarly standards. For me, it was the first direct order I had ever been given in a forty-year career.

But she was not quite finished. She was now on a high.

"We're a team!! We're a team!!" she screeched in her little-girl soprano before sweeping out of the tiny office and slamming the door behind her.

Things were obviously going to be difficult. I did debate going home, packing the bags and just getting a flight out. But that would be the action of a quitter and moreover, coming to Cyprus had been hellishly expensive. Cut one's losses or stay on and try to recoup some of the outlay? And, what is more, I now had a score to settle—or rather several scores if one counted all the ways we had been misled and deceived by the Institute. No, let's stay a little longer, Loydz and I agreed, and see what turns up. My wife, more optimistic than I am, believes that with the right mental attitude things will always turn out well. She is often right.

What was absolutely amazing was that any university, not just this, would allow a subject to be taught by someone with absolutely no experience or background or qualifications in it. To make such a person head of department in the subject with the freedom to issue orders to professionals teaching it, beggars belief. Management information systems as a subject is not, as one might think, one where no one will get hurt if a practitioner is not properly trained. Granted, an MIS amateur would not be as immediately dangerous as say, a badly trained heart surgeon. But that is not to say that workers in the field are exempt from the need to conform to carefully defined standards of professionalism and ethical behaviour, especially in this day and age when computer-based information systems lie at the heart of many of our life-critical support systems such as are used in agriculture, health care, energy supply, water distribution and more. To make a computer-illiterate chemist head of management information systems differs only in degree from firing the Director of Neurosurgery to make a job for the university president's teenage mistress, something which would not have been beyond the bounds of possibility had the regulating authorities been stupid enough to entrust the teaching of neurosurgery to the American Institute of Cyrpus.

This was the first of many encounters with her during the first term. I soon came to realise that TFC was one of those people who, while not totally dysfunctionally mentally unwell, was unable to take an objective view of the world and her role in it. I have met a number of them during my working life and without being any sort of psychiatrist, I perceive in them a hormonal lack of balance which causes a spontaneous overflow of irrational anger. This anger is often backed by considerable energy so that they often get into positions where they can inflict great unhappiness on other people. She was capable of functioning at work after a fashion. She was not really sick but she was not completely well either. Had her disability been physical rather than mental, everyone would have been very sympathetic. As it was, her temper tantrums, her spontaneous rages and her arrogance meant that she had, as far as I could perceive, not a single friend in the entire AIC, save the Dean and the Rector, who took advantage of her dependence on them by working her like a slave and giving her all sorts of those make-work irksome tasks which academic administrators are paid to invent and which they would never dare impose on real working teachers for fear of the reaction.

I could have made a fuss, gone to the Rector and made a formal complaint. But even after a few days in Kyrenia, I had already worked out the pointlessness of doing that. The option of cutting losses and getting a plane home is used by quite a few of the many new faculty members who arrive at the airport each September clutching contracts with the Institute. The heat, the local attitudes to foreigners, the delays in paying the low salaries and the high cost of living mean that many would-be teachers might stay for only a few days or weeks before putting Cyprus down to experience and moving on. The Institute was quite used to it and would therefore make more annual appointments than it had jobs to fill, knowing that there would be a fairly high initial attrition rate as well as a steady loss of faculty throughout the year.

Many of these turnarounds were used to living a sort of middle-aged hippy lifestyle. There is a special type of teacher who becomes a permanent expatriate. Their usual academic subject is English, or more accurately, English as a Foreign Language or EFL. Even though the Institute is nominally anglophone, the English of almost all the students and very many of the lecturers is poor to non-existent, so it employs a large cadre of English teachers. Students who do not speak English well enough must, in theory, learn it first by spending a full year studying nothing else. In this way, the AIC is no different from the literally hundreds or even thousands of schools and universities across Asia, Africa and South America which offer employment to teachers of EFL. The indigent, footloose EFL teacher with a taste for travel and no great materialistic expectations will have no trouble finding a secure, if lowly, berth in one of them, before moving on to an identical job in another. As a result, the expatriate EFL teacher has become an instantly identifiable species, a throwback to the 60's, lacking only the long hair and the guitar slung over the shoulder. Most of these latter day Jack Kerouac's stay for only a year or two. Here and there, though, were some who had set out on the hippy trail and found themselves bogged down far from home.

"Wouldn't you like to go back to England?" I asked one of these semi-permanent expatriates.

"I sure would," he replied, "but I can't afford the airfare."

How I missed my fully-equipped office in Heidelberg which I had been able to personalise with a wooden desk, leather chairs, an Afghan rug and with water colours and my diplomas on the walls. This was definitely the other end of the scale. I felt then, not for the last time, a sense of returning to my roots, that my working conditions had reverted to that time, decades earlier when, as a very junior lecturer, I had been at the very bottom of the pecking order when it came to my location in the staff room.

I have long believed that when you think you have reached the very bottom, look carefully and you will find a trapdoor to take you even lower. So, it came as something of a confirmation of this pessimistic philosophy when I found that my meagre and completely unprofessorial accommodation was to be shared, not just with my new colleague but with a family of mice who would emerge from the hole in the corner, which was a conduit to a broken drain, and brazenly run around the edges of the tiny room.

The English are a strange race and for many of them, animal welfare is the one single cause which will excite their latent emotions. Never mind all the injustices and cruelties in the world—many Englishmen (and women) will only ever feel anything approaching humanity at the thought of the suffering of some animal. Bull-fighting, for example, will anger them in a way that a million pictures of starving African children never could. When the House of Commons brought in a bill to abolish field sports, it unleashed a storm of public emotion while the simultaneous slaughter of thousands of Iraqi civilians was taking place as a casual unacknowledged backdrop.

But I, unlike most of my compatriots, have never been one to be sentimental about other species, so the problem of the mice had first to be confronted head-on. Traps are messy, a cat is impractical so it had to be poison and I immediately went to the supermarket to look for some. Clearly, we were not the only people with rodent problems because the shelves were full of traps and poisons and those sticky cards the mice get stuck on. A kilo of poisoned grain was duly purchased and poured into the hole in the corner and, apart from a bad smell for a week or two, the problem went away.

My first administrative task was to begin the dreaded registration. Every term students have to sign up for the courses they want to take. There are multiple conditions on exactly which courses they are actually allowed to take depending on their previous grades, the prerequisites of their intended courses and whether they are on academic probation or not. In most universities, this job, which is essentially clerical data input, would be done by secretarial staff or temporary employees such as senior students working a part-time job on campus thereby leaving the professoriat to less important tasks such as class preparation, course development, academic conferences or research. But not in AIC, where all of the faculty are roped in for the signing up of new and returning students. Naturally, during the registration period, all scholastic endeavour would be suspended. With the inevitable result that professors and lecturers would turn up for classes, when they eventually began, under—or unprepared.

The situation was especially acute in the Department of Management Information Systems. Each term there are some two hundred students to be signed up and, during my first week, there were just the two of us to do it, myself and Reban. Fortunately, I was informed by one of the students that the start of classes has been delayed because this year the registration period coincided with the last week of Ramadan. The end of Ramadan is a time for celebration and most of the student body would be home in Turkey until the first day of term. This meant that the lost registration week would be made up for by holding back the start of teaching for a further week.

This information had come from a reliable source, i.e. a student, so I could be sure it had filtered right down to the whole Institute, missing out only the members of the faculty, who were expected to acquire this sort of vital information by some invisible mechanism such as osmosis or air-borne bacteria. Memos informing teachers of this kind of important administrative change were rarely issued and never in advance. From time to time there might be some notice of a forthcoming change issued, in Turkish, after the date when it was supposed to be effective but this was not general and faculty had to depend heavily on the student grapevine for important information regarding schedules.

The extension of the registration period was a mixed blessing. On the one hand, it did mean that we have more time to register the huge number of students but on the other hand, most of the students would be staying at home in Turkey and would not be travelling to Cyprus until the day before the start of classes when lecturers would be required to register dozens of students in between teaching classes and lecture preparation.

Why, I hear you ask, did the AIC not invest in some decent software to permit online computer-based registration like most universities do these days? Well actually, it did have a sort of home-brew system. This is what the professors were expected to use to input the student data. But this software system, being home-made, was none-too-reliable. In addition to its many programming design faults it also had lots of errors in the records of student academic histories. Actually, the whole system leaked like a sieve and those responsible for registering students usually had to enroll the students manually as well as by computer and hope that the registrar, a very hard-working young man with a small team of helpers would be able to override all the software failures and reconcile the differing hand-written and electronic registration records.

Officially, students are encouraged to do their own registration online and that part of the system came equipped with a full set of instructions in Turkish and English. But students were afraid of the technology or did not trust it, the latter an understandable position in the AIC. Or they just couldn't be bothered-far easier to get a professor to do it for them. This mistrust of electronic operations is part of the culture both inside the AIC and in the wider Northern Cyprus community. For example, after a student has been entered into the online registration system, they were required to get four copies of their schedule of classes to be signed by the lecturer who had enrolled them. It used to be three copies—'everything in triplicate' is a holdover from the British colonial administration—but just to be on the safe side, let's take one extra. The lecturer kept two of these copies and hid them away just in case they were ever needed again, which they never were.

Four

So, the die was cast. Having come so far, we should at least try to make a go of it. The Institute would not be the whole of our existence and we could, perhaps, make a life in Cyprus for a short while at least. Going back to France would be like giving up too soon and we were also hoping to recover some of the large costs of the move. On a full professor's pay, we would have enough to feed and clothe ourselves so the decision was made to tough it out and to try to enjoy what is, scenically at least, a very beautiful island.

After a few days of catching our breath in the dormitory, we set out to look for an apartment. It was soon obvious that there was no shortage of habitation in the city. There had been a building boom for several years past and there were many empty flats. In addition, there were plenty of apartments bought as second homes by foreigners, mainly British, which were left empty for the winter. We were shown several and eventually settled on an apartment owned by a local Turkish landlord called Mr. Ozalay. We drew up a more or less standard contract with him with the help of a local estate agent and paid over to him a month's rent and two month's rent as a 'refundable' deposit.

The pound sterling was very strong at that time so Mr Ozalay insisted that we pay him in it. What is more he wanted the rent to be paid in cash every month, thus side-stepping the estate agent's commission. When previously renting apartments in other countries, the deposit had always been only one month's rent, not two. What's more, the rent would have been payable in the local currency and I would have arranged a standing order at the bank.

But then, this was Cyprus where several different currencies are in simultaneous use. If you want to buy an apartment or a car, then the transaction will be in pounds sterling cash, as will anything to do with renting property. Some items in the shops are traded in American dollars but the greenback is not usually used for everyday dealings. The common currency at the supermarket, for electricity, for water and for other everyday purchases such as taxis and restaurants, is the New Turkish Lira or YTL but this volatile, unstable currency is only ever used for small everyday transactions. Serious deals are always in hard currency, usually pounds or euros. Students must pay their tuition fees in euros even though the Institute pays its own costs in YTL. Institute salaries are in YTL for local Cypriot employees and a mixture of YTL and euros for foreigners like me.

With Mr Ozalay holding our eight hundred pounds deposit, we set up home in his apartment. It was named 'Ozyalcin' after one of the island's leading builders. Indeed, there were Ozyalcin Apartments everywhere. In the first two months we were there, we watched a couple of Ozyalcin apartment blocks arise before our very eyes across the street. The place was convenient for the Astro supermarket where we could buy substandard provisions at Fortnum and Mason prices and a local café, the CaféDaD, where we soon became regulars.

We slipped into a comfortable routine. Weekdays I would go into the Institute to teach my classes and on Saturday we would shop at Astro followed by a visit to CaféDaD where the owner, Albertin, was a football fan who showed British football on wide-screen TV. Having signed up for a deal with the local provider, Turkcell, we could also watch satellite BBC TV in the apartment. On Sundays, Loydz would go to the small local Roman Catholic church, a small concrete building designed in the Byzantine style and dedicated to St. Elizabeth of Hungary. There she quickly established herself as a reader to the congregation of British expatriates, holidaymakers and Nigerian students.

While she was at prayer, I would take a more spirituous fortification at the pretentious 1930's Dome Hotel. There I would read the English Sunday papers. In the summer *The Sunday Times* would arrive on Sunday but after the start of November, when many of the British had gone home, the only newspaper usually available would be *The Daily Mail*, except very occasionally when other British papers might be obtained a day late.

After Loydz had finished her devotions, she would meet up with me and we would go off to a good lunch. There are quite a few decent restaurants in the town. During summer, a dozen or more open-air restaurants around the famously picturesque harbour offered excellent sea-food but even after the tourists had left, many excellent restaurants stayed open throughout the short cool winter. One need not go hungry in Northern Cyprus—the catering is usually first class whether it be simple snacks at street cafes or a slap-up meal at a top-quality restaurant. For Loydz and I, Sunday lunch, always at a different place, was the high spot of our week.

I had been ordered by TFC to teach the elementary statistics class along with my three evening graduate classes. After nearly fifty years of working with computer systems, I have some experience of how they work, what is important about them and what we should pass on about them to the next student generation. I made one last attempt to get her to change my timetable to something more appropriate to my experience. I told her once again that although I had previously taught introductory statistics, it was a waste of my time when so many mainstream courses in information systems did not have a teacher and the faculty was swarming with statistics teachers.

'The Dean has appointed me Head of MIS and it is my decision what you will teach!'

And with that she did her impersonation of Violet Elizabeth Bott, quite literally stamping her foot and storming out of the room.

Fortunately, I had brought with me an elementary statistics textbook and I was able to start preparation. My three graduate classes were more like what I was used to—a survey course on management information systems, a course of programming using the Java programming language and a course on database management.

The master's degree was satisfying to teach. The students were cosmopolitan and all had a good grounding in English. Most of them had graduated from universities outside Cyprus and some, particularly the Iranians, come with very sound technical backgrounds indeed. The basic degree offered by the Faculty of Graduate Studies was the MBA with specialisation in one of several subjects, including economics, law or international relations as well as MIS.

The first week or so was when the students, both graduate and undergraduate, would drift in. They would extend their summer break until, I guess, their fathers got sick of seeing them around the house and pack them off to college. It was not a good idea to try to teach anything in the first week because the class would often be less than half-full and whatever material was discussed in class would need to be reprised in the next couple of weeks as the class personnel changed.

While the graduate students were from a variety of countries—Iran, Nigeria, India, the central Asian republics, etc.—the undergraduate students were almost all from Turkey, with only a 10% or so leavening of Cypriots and foreigners. This meant that language difficulties formed a large part of the teaching challenge. As an Englishman, I had no choice but to speak to them in English but the Turkish educational system, while producing many good anglophone professionals, does not make English, the world's most widely-used language, a central part of the curriculum for its primary—or secondary—school pupils. In many countries, fluency in English is considered a necessary prerequisite for a professional career, and every pupil studies it. But not in Turkey. I imagine that, since the Turkish educational establishment does not mandate the teaching of English, it is because they are waiting for the day when the rest of the world abandons English and adopts Turkish as the standard medium for trade, finance, international travel and culture. As a result of their lack of any knowledge of the world's most important commercial language, the students of the Institute were not able, for the most part, to make the classes any sort of two-way dialogue. This puts an enormous strain on the teacher, who must keep talking for up to three hours as well as writing everything on the whiteboard. Turkish-speaking faculty would sometimes cheat by giving all or part of the class in the local language, although this was officially frowned upon because as well as inhibiting the student's learning of English, it alienates the minority of 'foreign' students in the class whose hard-currency fees are so critical to the Institutes's business plan.

Another problem was the availability of textbooks. It is common practice in American universities to base the whole content of a course around a particular textbook. Indeed, there is a very large and profitable publishing industry centred around American academia which is dedicated to supplying textbooks tailored to standard nationally accepted syllabi. To give one example, every American college student is required to take a course called 'College Algebra'. The syllabus for College Algebra is set by national committee and what is taught is pretty much the same in every degree-awarding college from Bangor, Maine to San Diego, California.

While it is not exactly an endorsement of the much-trumpeted virtues of academic freedom, the system does allow the easy transfer of students and their credits from one institution to another. The whole process of getting standard books in American universities is therefore completely streamlined. The publishers' representatives would liaise with lecturers and professors to arrange for the right number of copies to be delivered to the on-campus bookstore for the start of term. To deter the growth of a second-hand market in standard textbooks, publishers would simply re-arrange the layout of the material in the book every two years and announce a new, improved, and more expensive edition, which would be more or less the same as the old edition but with all the content in different places. Newer editions of textbooks in contemporary subjects such as computing would be updated with more recent material, but the syllabus for College Algebra mentions nothing discovered later than 1800, so a new edition can be put together quickly, and profitably, via simple cutting and pasting.

By contrast, the traditional, liberal attitude of British universities has been to indicate a list of textbooks which students could read or not read as they fancy. With no prescribed book, the students would be forced to make their own way through material which would be eventually served up at the final examination. This worked perfectly well when universities were, by definition of their exclusivity, centres of excellence. But in these democratic times of mass education, when a university degree is no longer a badge of intellectual distinction but has become just another middle-class consumer possession, the old Oxbridge-based way of doing things simply will not work. The modern student in the learning factory must be spoon-fed with bite-sized chunks of learning material from standard textbooks, supporting DVD's, online backup material, lists of websites etc. etc. The job of the modern university teacher is often only to guide a large class of students through this forest of material.

So when I asked TFC, perhaps naively, what we were to do about textbooks, she told me, with her customary asperity, to go find some free e-books i.e. books published online and available in what the Institute preciously called its 'Cybrary', a computer room full of desktop PC's where electronic 'resources' could be accessed. Lecturers were told to stipulate a textbook for a particular course, but there was no guarantee that the Cybary or the library would have a copy of it or would even be able to get hold of one. Students could order their own copies of standard books via *amazon.com* or some other online bookseller or even through the Institute bookshop itself, but delivery to Northern Cypus was slow and expensive, so students rarely bothered.

So what did students at AIC do for books? Photocopying, that's what. At the Institute 'bookstore'. It wasn't a bookshop in the usual sense of the term, of course. Sure, there were a few Turkish novels languishing on the shelves, limp from the heat, and here and there, if one looked carefully, one might uncover a wilting version of the Windows 98 User Manual. But usable textbooks, no. The bookstore was actually the home of half a dozen industrial strength photocopiers of which three were continuously dedicated to the copying of textbooks. As one who has only previously lived in countries where the copyright laws were observed, I was shocked to see one of my elderly colleagues, a full professor, carefully making multiple photocopies of a hard-back standard text as a normal part of his course preparation.

This insouciance with regard to the copyright laws as they apply in, say, the European Union, is particularly Turkish Cypriot. Not just books, but the latest films illegally copied on DVD are available at four for 10 YTL or one could buy a fake Rolex watch or phoney Prada handbag at several stores on the town's main street. It is unlikely that the local traders in fakes have any conscience about what they are doing. Indeed, they unconsciously display a quite touching naivety when they are flogging their stuff. For example, if you ask the price of the fake Louis Vuitton bag they will give you some unrealistic price such as two hundred pounds, as if it were the genuine article on sale at a bargain price. Now, even I, a mere male, know that you can't buy a real LV handbag for only two hundred pounds—they cost very much more. On the other hand, I also know that a genuine, plausible far-eastern Louis Vuitton fake will set you back no more than $20 from a sidewalk stall in Manila or Taiwan.

The other event during the first week of classes was the official opening ceremony attendance at which was compulsory for all teaching staff. Full academic dress, no less. Naturally, when one is wearing a dark suit and a full-length academic gown, it is just the right day for the summer heat-wave to return to summon up its last assault before it cedes its place to the slightly cooler Cyprus autumn. So in a temperature of about 35C and dressed as for a degree day ceremony at a British university on a mild June afternoon, we made our way to the large hall where assorted dignitaries, including the Minister of Education of the Turkish Republic of Northern Cyprus, were waiting to address us in Turkish. One senior member of the Institute did make a speech extolling the virtues of learning and speaking English as a career-advancing necessity but he was only listened to in polite silence and given only lukewarm applause. There was then some music and a trio of musicians stepped up to play two pieces, both French, on guitars and clarinet. It is difficult to understand why both pieces were funeral music—Fauré's '*Elegy*' and Ravel's '*Pavane for a Dead Infanta*'. But the two popular pieces were competently played, the plangent clarinet being ideally suited to their haunting *tristesse* made all the more poignant by the unconscious inclusion of a liberal sprinkling of oriental quarter tones.

The second week of term brought up a new problem, the problem of getting the immigation papers.

"It is no problem." the Human Resources Department assured me, "we will help you."

"Help me?" I thought, "In every other university abroad that I"ve worked in, I have had it done for me."

But no, not here. They explained the procedure to me. I would need, they told me, a work permit and a certificate of residency. This would not be easy and they are expensive. The first thing would be to get a blood test and, most important, to bring the results back to the HR Department without breaking the seal. Presumably this is so that someone carrying a dangerous blood disorder will not substitute the results from a healthy person.

"Please pay 30 YTL." said the young woman from HR.

I went with Loydz to get my blood test at the specially-recommended laboratory which has an exclusive deal with the Institute for faculty blood-letting. After ascertaining that I was who I said I was—the Institute lent me back my passport for this—and that I was indeed a bona fide member of the AIC, I was ready to yield up a few millilitres.

The slim young nurse dabbed my left arm with spirit and tried to find the vein. Three times. Finally she gave up and sent for her boss, a slightly less young, slightly less slim but definitely physically stronger woman. The second woman rolled up my right sleeve and prepared to give me a matching pair of bruises. Alas, the vein on my right arm would not give itself up to penetration either. So in frustration at my, or rather my vein's, lack of co-operation, a third, and decidedly bigger and very much stronger, colleague was sent for. This large new woman preferred the left arm, so she went back to it, determined to finish the job. Finally after much effort, a phial full of my lifeblood was extracted. The whole process had sent Loydz running from the room by the second try but she recovered sufficiently to pay them 80 YTL on my behalf, the results to be picked up a couple of days later. I resisted the temptation to look at what they had to say about me until after I had turned over the sealed envelope to HR.

"We need the receipt," said HR.

"Why?"

"For the police."

'The police?"

"Yes, the police need the receipt."

'The receipt, not the medical report?"

"No, only the receipt. The report has to go to immigration in Lefkosa."

"Is this a health check or some convoluted accountancy scam?" I wondered.

But since I and not the AIC, had paid for the test, I felt I was entitled to see what was in it. Surprisingly, what exercises the public health officials of the TRNC, are not those notifiable serious diseases carried in the bloodstream by visitors to foreign parts such as cholera, yellow fever, trypanosomas, denguie fever, smallpox etc. No, only the sexual diseases were tested for—syphilis, gonorrhea, HIV and so on. I suppose it is symptomatic of a puritan culture that these would be what frighten them the most. I was later told by a long-term expatriate that I was lucky that local health checks had advanced to the stage where they no longer required an anal scrape before they would give you a work permit.

I paid HR the remaining 190 YTL for my work permit and then addressed part two of the problem: how to get a resident's permit for Loydz, who would not be working because she could not get a decent job and being a Filipina, the only job she would ever be offered would be menial work in a hotel. As a long-term university teacher, I know that her intellect and her university degree are superior to those of a great many of my students but, on the other hand, she is from The Philippines, which is unalterable. It is a bland assumption that racial prejudice is something which rich white Europeans invented and exported to the world. This is a convenient myth with which to beat citizens of former imperial countries who are expected to feel an unforgivable colonial guilt. In reality my wife and I have continually to endure the kind of institutional racism which she is subjected to every time she is aggressively interrogated by a public official, especially an immigration policemen of whatever nationality, as well as the tacit racist unspoken assumption that the only work a Filipina graduate is fit for is menial work.

"Your wife's residency should be easier than a work permit." said HR, "Obviously a blood test first. Be sure to keep the receipt for the police and, most important, bring the report back unopened."

Remembering the mangling of my arms a few days before, Loydz was understandably apprehensive. Scars and bruises on the hairy male arm can look quite macho, but the butchering of smooth hairless womanly skin, softened to perfection as it usually is by a lifetime of creams and unguents, is a different matter altogether. But the youngest and slimmest of the impaling trinity extracted the blood effortlesly. When we came to pick up the report and pay, the clerk said, without a trace of a blush,

'That will be 100 YTL.'

"But you only charged my husband eighty!"

"Yes, that is because he is a member of AIC."

The clerk's register was open and Loydz saw a long unbroken column of 80's.

'They are all eighty.'

"Yes, of course. That's right. We charge eighty for Cypriots and a hundred for foreigners."

'That's not fair!"

"What's wrong with it? We always charge more for foreigners."

"Well eighty is all you are getting from me."

And she stuck to her guns and that is what she finished up paying.

That was only stage one of the process. We went back to HR to ask what we did next.

"You need a signed form from the Muhtar and then you need to go to the police to get a photograph and fill out the standard form. You will need to take both passports plus photocopies of the main pages. They will need to see your entry visa to TRNC and you will also need to pay the money at the police station."

"Is that all?"

"No, after you get the form back from the police, come back here and we will take the form to the immigration head office in Lefkosa. We have a motor bike which goes every day. Bring 10 YTL for his petrol."

"What is this 'Muhtar'?"

Here the HR Director consulted her Turkish-English dictionary.

"He's the village headman. He has to sign that you are living in the city."

"Where do I find him?"

"He has a café opposite the post office. Just ask. Everyone knows him. Be sure to take your passports and the tenancy agreement for your flat."

So we went down to the post office and, sure enough, across the road from it was one of the dirtiest cafés we had ever seen. The sort of place that gives squalor a bad name. And inside was the Muhtar. We told him what we wanted.

"Come back tomorrow!" he ordered.

His manners were as black as his fingernails.

"You can't do it now?"

'Tomorrow!"

So after wasting an hour and an expensive taxi ride, we had no choice but to go back the next day.

The next day he was open for business. He took only a cursory look at our passports and tenancy document and then dashed off a form. The whole process took about one minute. He was probably in a hurry because he had other clients waiting: we saw him write about four forms in the five minutes we were there.

'Ten!" and we duly handed over the note.

As rackets go, this is a real beaut.—selling meaningless forms to foreigners. I wondered why the police don't close him down? An unworthy thought, of course. If the police closed him down they would lose a nice little earner and they would therefore be forced to increase their own prices, something which would be difficult to do because the prices listed in the police station had been officially fixed by the Ministry of Bribes and Backhanders.

So now off to the police station with all our bits of paper, including the Muhtar's pink form and our receipt for Loydz' blood test. The police station was halfway out of town well-hidden at the end of a long street. Inside, Loydz was photographed and money changed hands—about 250 YTL or £100—and after more forms, we were told to come back next week when her passport would be ready. After the second trip a week later, we got a piece of paper to send to the head office at Lefkosa via the motorbike.

Total cost of getting work and residence permits? About 750 YTL (or $600 or £300) and about twenty hours of trudging from office to office.

All this money going out and still no salary coming in. It was by now mid-October and we had been in Cyprus for over a month. I had earned half a month's salary—approximately €1100-for September, but the Institute, as well as being reluctant to pay promptly before its student tuition fees had been taken in, also operated a weird policy of paying only one third of the salary at the end of the working month and the other two thirds in the middle of the following month. What is more, the first third is paid in YTL and only the second two-thirds is paid in euros. I never found out whether this arrangement applies equally to both locals and foreigners although I was told that local faculty and other staff are only paid in YTL with no euro component, which would have been a waste of hard currency. But it does mean that one is always working six or more weeks in arrears and that makes it impossible to take up a job at AIC without substantial savings or a second, back-up income-in my case, my British pension.

I came across a similar way of doing things when, in 1981, I worked for a small computer consultancy which leased my services to Shell Nigeria. At that time we also got paid in a similar one third/two thirds mixture of Nigerian naira and some hard currency such as British pounds or Dutch guilders. A few judicious hacks into the IBM mainframe soon showed up the scam—since only the oil companies had access to western currency with which they paid the leasing company, it was an almost perfect way of turning soft, non-convertible naira into something that could be put into a London bank in preparation for the day when the next scheduled military coup would force our company's bosses to make a quick exit on the London plane.

When AIC classes began properly, the undergraduate course in statistics proved as unpleasant and difficult to teach as TFC had planned it would be. Every Friday afternoon, a subset of the class attendance would gather to re-learn the statistics they had failed to learn the year before when the teacher had been no less than TFC herself. It was, of course, a different subset each week, apart from a small core of real students who would try vainly to learn something against a backdrop of constant Turkish chatter from the rest, who would arrive late and disappear at regular intervals for self-awarded smoke breaks. I never had more than twenty-five students present at any one time. Indeed, I had to wait until the midterm exam to learn that the class was supposed to have nearly fifty signed-up students.

My other classes—of MBA students were, by contrast, more like I was used to-classes of manageable size made up of students fluent in English. Graduate classes were all held in the evenings which had the advantage that one could go home by the Institute shuttle bus which left each evening at 9.00 pm and passed just by our apartment.

For the first couple of weeks of term, TFC left me alone but as the weeks went by she grew into her role as head of department. Indeed, she may have started to believe that she really was a proper professional MIS academic and she began to assert herself.

She started, for example, to come into the office and to ask Reban and me to drop whatever we were doing and adjourn to her office for a 'meeting'. She would do this even when I was in a discussion with a student or even a senior faculty colleague. I tried to reason with her that I was at that moment busy in consultation with maybe, the Dean of Graduate Studies, but she would hear nothing of it.

"Come to my office! Now!" she would demand, her face puce with rage.

To his good-natured credit, the Dean of Graduate Studies was well-aware of her personal manner and would demur with well-mannered grace.

These meetings were often something and nothing—a pep-talk about getting grades in on time, for example. Although sometimes they were excuses for her to give us some new orders. One of these was an instruction to rewrite substantial portions of our lecture notes for a distance, i.e. online, education course she had cooked up in an effort to impress the Rector. I raised the question of the need for there to be some discussion before such a major undertaking were entered into, given our limited departmental resources. I have had some experience of teaching computer-based subjects over the Internet and I know just how difficult and resource-hungry they can be. All I could see was an open-ended responsibility with little positive payoff and a great deal of fruitless hard work which I had certainly not signed up for.

Well, that's what I thought and I was about to explain it to TFC when she went ballistic and the meeting was over.

"I am getting very angry!!" she screamed, loud enough for half the AIC campus to hear.

She subsequently referred to my insubordination at another of her 'meetings' when she tried the 'more in sorrow than anger' method of trying to shame me for my lack of cooperation. Unfortunately, she was not very good at sorrow, her forte was anger. So sorrowful morphed swiftly into irate, a predictable mood I was now well used to.

Another of her ploys was to demand to see copies of my CV on a weekly basis. She would demand that I make random changes to it. For example, after I had added to it my new responsibilities as a teacher on the MBA programme, she insisted that I remove them. On another occasion she told me to rearrange my publications list by international, national and other categories.

"It's the way we do it here," she said.

"And I will be looking at all your so-called publications. We have a big database in Turkey where we can check them all."

She also removed my reference to one of my old publications on software complexity. Admittedly it was only a slight effort, creatively speaking, but it was surely mine own and I am not sure she had the right to ask me to erase it. But given the eccentric interpretation of what passes for scholarly endeavour in Northern Cyprus, who knows, it might be perfectly normal practice?

TFC's behaviour could be laughed off as that of an eccentric and her wilder demands could have been ignored were it not for two things—her immediate recourse to anger in response to any human interaction and her malevolent use of her political connexions both inside and outside the AIC. It was known that she had been shifted from department to department as she had accumulated enemies. And, it was rumoured, she was fire-proof because of her rich mother's regular donations to certain personnel. How true that particular rumour might be is questionable but it is certainly true that such stories were quite plausible given the flexible morality of Nothern Cyprus where absolute honesty is not nearly as important as loyalty and obligation to one's family and friends.

The first major breach in the uneasy peace between us came when TFC took on the task of selecting students for the MIS PhD programme, something which had been on my own job description. A student who had recently graduated with his master's degree was looking to advance to the doctorate. For some reason to do with the substratum of dubious local politics which would always be opaque to me, this particular young man had incurred the violent hatred of TFC which is not, in itself, a very difficult accomplishment. She came to tell me about him when Reban was out of the office.

"He must, must NOT be allowed to join the PhD programme!! NO!! NO!! NO!! NEVER!!" she screamed in her infantile voice like an overweight, grotesque spoilt child, all the while striding around the room thumping the desks.

"He is a liar, a LIAR!! He bribed his way to his degree!! He cheated in his exams!! He just wants to do a PhD to stay out of the army!! He is a very bad man and we must never let him into the PhD program!!" And so she ranted on.

I told her that I could not support her on the basis of her allegations alone. Indeed, it is the usual practice to exercise due process in student applications at all levels. Her prejudice would not, and should not, be enough to keep a student out of the Institute. Even, I pointed out, mass-murderers are allowed a fair hearing. In the end I offered to join with an interview panel for the applicant the following week and to design an aptitude exam for him. I wrote the exam and drew up a list of interview questions.

Of course, this interview and exam did not take place. Instead, on the day before they were scheduled, TFC called Reban and me, together with another faculty member from outside the department, to a hastily convened meeting where she once again went through her routine of vilifying our student applicant. At the end, Reban and the other man succumbed to her pressure and she drew up a statement excluding the applicant from the Institute, defence case unheard. I refused to sign it and instead issued my own dissenting opinion that due process should have been carried out which I sent to the AIC authorities including the Graduate Admissions Committee.

My disobedience did not go unpunished, of course. After pointedly snubbing me for a week or so, she sent me a memo regretting that I had disturbed departmental harmony by my personal attack on her. It was nothing of the sort but then she would never be able to develop the correct academic detachment to understand proper civilised behaviour.

Because of my *lèse-majesté*, I was immediately removed by her from all my administrative duties regarding the graduate students and my opprobrium was further intensified when the decision of her *ad hoc* committee was overturned by the Graduate Executive Council who admitted the student applicant on to the PhD programme after all. One of her retaliations to this public insult was that I was no longer allowed to review applications for admission to the MBA and PhD programmes even though I was still the only professor qualified to teach at the graduate level. She, as an assistant professor, was officially disqualified by AIC rules. Not that this made any difference to her view of her own duties in this matter. She arranged with her patron, the Dean, and with the Faculty Secretary that all graduate applications would no longer come to me but would be sent directly to her—thus effectively cutting out of the loop. If a second signature were needed she would involve Reban, who, for various personal reasons, was not in a position to take a stand.

Five

By November the weather in Cyprus turns much cooler and for someone from a cold wet country, the change is welcome. In fact, November daytime temperatures hover around 20C, which is what we Britons call warm. But it did mean that we would need blankets on the bed and a sweater in the evening. By now I felt comfortable wearing working suits and I could switch off the office airconditioning.

This is the season of the year when the Institute enacts the great ceremony of The Mid Term Examinations. As a long-time teacher in American universities, I was used to setting midterm examinations in one of my regular class periods. This is a quick and efficient way of doing it. One tells the students 'midterm next week', prepares it, sets it and then grades it afterwards. No problem.

That is not the way we do it here, I was told by the Faculty Secretary. All the exams are held at a scheduled time and place and lectures are suspended for about two weeks so that lecturers can invigilate their own and others' examinations. It is the system used in large British universities where classes may have hundreds of students. Some classes in the Institute did indeed have large numbers, but all my classes were comparatively small, usually never more than forty officially signed up, so I could quite easily have run my own exams. But, I was also informed, the Institute has no say in the matter: the format is mandated by YOD and YODAK, the ministries of education in Ankara and Lefkosa respectively.

The problem with setting aside an extended period solely for midterm examinations, apart from the loss of teaching time it entails, which some lecturers enjoy, of course, is that it means that the exams spill over into the weekends and evenings. Somehow the taking of an exam at say, 8.00 pm on a Saturday or Sunday evening, offends against one's sense of there being a proper time and place for everything. I was certainly not convinced that it was a good idea that I should go to the Institute for just one hour at 4.00 pm on a Saturday so that I could invigilate an examination about the national history of Turkey. Another aggravation during the exam period was that the Institute's shuttle bus service was rearranged to an even more erratic schedule than usual. So one hour's invigilation not only ruined a day I could have spent on research or relaxation but also cost me taxi fares both there and back.

The main duty of the exam invigilator is to stop the students from cheating. We were required to deliver a little homily on the virtues of honesty before we started and during the exam we were expected to keep our eyes open to the many ingenious tricks the students would get up to. Such was the prevalence of academic dishonesty during the exams that I couldn't help thinking that the Cypriot culture of cheating is so deeply ingrained that we, those invigilators who try to impose alien standards of academic self-reliance, are the ones who are missing the point.

The taking of closed-book written examinations to be answered independently by the student so that his teachers can assess how much he has learned is a peculiarly western concept. The Turkish—or other oriental student often does not see this process as natural at all. Indeed, the idea is completely alien to him. For the Turkish majority of students at the Institute, the first priority in the student-teacher relationship is to help one's friends. The teacher is an adversary who is withholding what the student wants i.e. the right grade so that he can progress to the diploma. There is no notion in their philosophy of any concept of individual effort and if the teacher is to be successfully hoodwinked into awarding the required grade then it is best done by a team effort. So, in this war of attrition, the students would need to develop complex strategies for tricking the opposition. The idea that plagiarism or copying is somehow 'wrong', or dishonest, simply does not occur to them—that idea is as remote from their thinking as the Theory of Relativity would have been to a caveman in the Stone Age. For them, cooperation is the best way of both fooling the invigilator while, at the same time, discharging one's duty to one's friends. Not to meet this group obligation would be a serious dereliction of one's social duty which might very well lead to the penalty of long-term ostracism from a valuable support network.

This puts the invigilators in a very difficult position. Their job is not merely to try to prevent the students from copying from each other and whatever crib sheets they have secreted about their persons but they are also trying to overturn deep-seated cultural attitudes as well. I would guess that as few as 40% of exam answers were provided entirely honestly by English standards. And it is entirely possible that we, those of us who have grown up believing that one must take an exam oneself without help, who are on the wrong side of the argument in this fundamental cultural difference.

It goes deeper than mere custom. For while a Turk will be absolutely scrupulous in his dealings with a friend or family member, he feels absolutely no moral imperative at all to extend those scruples to an authority figure like a college teacher or indeed someone with whom he is doing business. One simply works with one's friends to leverage one's personal advantage because a time will come when your friends will do the same for you. And, in its way, this replacement of individual effort by a reliance on cooperation forms a perfectly consistent moral philosophy even if it is different from the one which westerners are used to.

The measures which students would go to in order to fool the invigilators were often extremely ingenious. In my subject, I rarely need to set examinations with essay-type written answers. The answers to my exam questions require real knowledge and the ability to write some computer code, or to solve some mathematical problem. Even so, the students would have tricks that I could not work out and I would frequently get the same wrong answers with the same punctuation mistakes from students sitting at opposite ends of the room and with their mobile phones removed. It was like being in the presence of a master conjurer.

The mobile phone, which is ubiquitous in Cyprus because of the near-impossibility of getting a fixed phone line, has been a great boon to the exam cheaters. Not only can students get text messages from other students in the class but also from friends on the outside. However vigilant the invigilator, it is impossible to monitor everyone in the room all the time. The mobile phone can also be used to download answers from the Internet or to store the classroom notes. During my first midterm exam invigilation at the Institute, one student was caught with an entire set of course notes, 150 kilobytes in all, stored on his cellphone.

Of course, traditional, low-tech cheating also goes on. If an invigilator looks at the left of the room, for example, there will be low-level muttering, impossible to locate, from the right and vice-versa. Another popular method used by students at AIC is to write the course notes in very small writing on lightweight paper and then fold them up to postage stamp size which can be cupped in the free hand.

And then there is the famous old 'girl friend's photo' trick. The student has a photo of a young woman which he consults from time to time 'for inspiration'. The lecture notes are underneath the photo, of course.

To combat the highly organised teams of exam cheats was a difficult task for the invigilators but they would have a number of techniques at their disposal. For example, suspected straightforward copying could be countered by simply moving the students to seats a long way apart although usually this would merely give the student a new neighbour to copy from. Temporary confiscation of the cellphones sometimes worked but students would rarely rely on a single technique but would come equipped with several backup plans should one of them be discovered.

One cunning plan came to light when lecturers were asked to use only special examination writing paper on which the Institute's seal had been rubber-stamped. However, the students proved amazingly ingenious at acquiring, i.e. stealing, sheets of the paper which had been already stamped. Answers to expected exam questions would be written on the ready-stamped writing paper for smuggling into the exam room. This trick only came to light when an alert invigilator noticed that students were handing in exam answers on paper slightly different in size from that which had been distributed.

Invigilators would also usually need to work in pairs to police different parts of the room: these pairs always included both English and Turkish speakers to listen for the mutterings.

Unfortunately, the invigilators themselves would sometimes unwittingly contribute to the copying culture. After the class had settled down, it was quite common for the author of the exam to make some announcement e.g.

"Stop please! Stop writing and listen to me! The word 'national' in Question 4 should be 'international'." or some such.

This was the signal for a general open negotiation between students and lecturer which would have questions and assertions flying backwards and forwards while the rest of the class muttered to each other, passed notes and used their cellphones in the confusion.

If he were not one of the invigilators himself, the teacher who had actually set the exam would sometimes pay a visit to the exam room specially to make this kind of announcement which they would also need to explain and amplify.

"When it says 'national' it really should say 'international' because the context of the question is about internationalism and globalisation and not just about national interests or I would have written the question differently. So cross out 'national' and write 'international' and answer the question from an international and not a national point of view. Is that clear?"

Of course, this announcement was insultingly pointless given that the question would be so self-explanatory—maybe something along the lines of—

'Is NATO a national organisation?'

Yes, the questions were often that short and simple. What is more, the lecturers would set the same questions term after term and never bother to rewrite the exam or even rephrase the questions. But every time the exam was held there would be some such announcement which would be the sign for students to create an open-floor dialogue.

"Excuse me professor, is that 'international' and not 'national'?"

"Yes, 'international' in place of 'national'."

By this time half the students would be shouting at the teacher and at each other and comparing answers on their exam sheets.

"But I've already written 'national'. Am I wrong?"

"No, he said 'international'."

"But I wrote 'national'. Will it affect my grade? I have an A so far!"

And this babble would continue for five minutes or so until until it petered out in resentful muttering as the students continued their private discussions.

"He did. That's what he said. He said 'international' instead of 'national'!!"

What always surprised me was that this type of break in proceedings for an animated discussion took place during every single exam, sometimes more than once.

The exams in economics or social science or politics were usually brief to the point of terseness. I was once asked to invigilate an exam which consisted of exactly 54 words of questions, including the titles. Three or four single sentence questions pitched at about GCSE level to be answered in 45 minutes was normal. I often wondered why the exam-setters didn't ever edit these minimalist exercises. In those 54 words, and admittedly that was the very shortest of all the exams I had the pleasure of invigilating—usually the exams ran to well over a hundred words of text—I counted eleven spelling and grammatical mistakes.

Invigilators did have some sanctions and could expel a student from the exam by writing the word "CHEAT" on the paper together with their signature. Students so outed would usually leave with a good grace, knowing that that was as far as the punishment would go—and they could always extend their college career by retaking the course later. But the ultimate sanction, expulsion from AIC, was never used. This sanction, which would be applied in many western universities, certainly for serious cases, carries, in Cyprus, much more than the loss of an academic career and a blot on a personal record. Turkey and Turkish Cyprus still have standing armies and conscription. Every young man is obliged to do twelve months national service and going to universiy is a way of avoiding, or at least deferring it. Many young men at the Institute will draw out their academic career to the best part of a decade which explains why so many students are happy to take failing grades and do the necessary course retakes. The Institute is also reluctant to discipline students by expelling them for the minor peccadillo of academic dishonesty since the students are paying good money to be there. Being sent down would condemn the young man to a year on a cold mountain on the Iraq border when he could have been dragging out his schooling to the advantage of all, with the possible exception of the recruiting sergeant. So, while it is undoubtedly true that a few exemplary expulsions would solve the cheating epidemic at a stroke and since the Institute will not apply the only sanction that will work, it is logical to assume that the Institute is quite happy with the situation as it is—a happy pretence that lecturers are controlling the universal practice of exam dishonesty while denying them the means to do anything about it.

I, personally, take a fairly robust approach to cheating. First, my subject is not one where the exam will centre on questions requiring the regurgitation of lecture notes so I point out that if they are going to copy from each other, they must be sure not to copy from someone who knows even less than they do. Then I explain my grading system in the event that I find out that the copying of an exam or a homework has taken place. I preface this with a little speech about how I came by my method.

First, I tell them that when I was a very young and pompous lecturer faced with two identical term papers, I would divide the marks between the two, so that an 80% paper appearing twice would give the two students 40% each. This is obviously unfair, so when I became more experienced as a grader of student efforts, I would try to arbitrate between two identical answers to determine who had really done the work and who had not. In many cases, this would be obvious because of the fluency of the handwriting and because of my knowledge of the students' comparative abilities and work-rate. I would then give all the marks to the original creator of the work and none to the copyist. But this meant, because I am not infallible, that the cheating student could still stand some chance of getting a good grade, even if the odds on that were not good. Finally, when I became old and cynical and I finally realised that rough justice will achieve things which careful reasoning will not, I hit on the system which I use now which is to award all the points for the duplicate homework or exam question to the student who has made the copy and none to the originator of the work who is therefore punished for his stupidity in letting his work be copied and who will subsequently not allow himself to be copied from in the future.

But in these days of photocopying and word-processing, it is usually not possible to identify the original author of a piece of homework or a term paper when all copies, original or derivative, look the same. My method still works though. When I see a piece of work for the first time, I grade it fairly, after which further identical copies of the same exercise are given some notional grade, say 10%. To be sure of being credited with a fair grade for having done the work first, the original author must make sure that his effort is the first to be read.

I explain this grading policy to all my classes at the start of the semester and it is amusing to see students fighting to be the last to hand in a homework so that theirs will be the first off the stack. That is why I shuffle the scripts before I start grading.

I could quite easily just 'go with the flow' by trying not to take the job seriously. I could have done what some of my colleagues would do and just turn a blind eye to student cheating. To do so would neither secure nor imperil my employment in an organisation which will fire an employee in a heartbeat. But I was recruited to the job as an academic mercenary and being a 'hired gun' brings with it a higher obligation of integrity than that expected of an established secure employee. I was also aware that I was being watched for any slippage in my standards so my view of the endemic academic dishonesty was to support the Institute's official stated position that they were against it. Even though, in practice, they did everything possible to make sure it flourished.

If they were ever to sort the problem out by returning academic cheaters to the hard world outside and a spell in the Turkish Army, then they would have had my whole-hearted support. The Turkish Army is after all, one of the great bastions of NATO and it plays a vital role in the defence of the eastern flank of the western world. I do not see it as part of my job to undermine the strength of the Turkish Army by manipulating exam grades so that the scholastically bereft student can escape his military obligations.

As a safety net for students who were too stupid even to cheat their way through the exams, the Institute offered a scheme called 'the Graduation Makeup Exam" by which students who had an F—a fail or a D minus on their record, can take, for a further payment (of course), a special exam to improve the grade. Students will often opt to take this exam in the innocent belief that the setter of the exam will take pity on their being so close to graduation and pass them on the nod so that they can pick up their diploma.

One such was Mehmet, who came to me with a sob story.

"Professor, I have to take graduation makeup now. My father, he say, Mehmet, you must pass this course with A or you must leave AIC. Professor it is very difficult. If I leave, I must go in army and I leave here my girlfriend. So you see, Professor, it is ver', ver' important for my life that I get A for this course." and with that he gave me the ingratiating smarmy smile of the crooked estate agent which he probably thought would win me over but in actuality just irritated me all the more.

He took the exam and his performance was a shade worse than dreadful so I gave it the over-generous grade of D minus. Maybe I had missed one of the unspoken rules that the accepted practice is that, in order to balance the books, everyone is supposed to pass the graduation makeup exam whether they have learned to walk upright or not. Little did Mehmet know that I had actually done him a very good turn indeed. I had, I hoped he realised, released him from his pathetic delusion that he possessed any intellectual talent whatsoever. He could very well, with those abilities, have a glittering career in the Turkish Army. The military needs more people like him.

By now I was starting to understand the way AIC was run. It was, like most of the country's universities,'private'. Indeed, TFC had made much of its status, as if it were a private university in the style of famous American private universities like Harvard or Yale, or if not quite so prestigious, at least on a par with some exclusive midwestern private liberal arts college. Not so. An American private university is not usually a business run for profit. While it is true that a good private American school will indeed take its income from (usually high) fees and supplement its capital value by the charitable donations of its wealthy alumni, it will usually be able to offer good value for money. Faculty salaries will be attractive to the best international academics and academic standards will be maintained by rigorous accreditation monitoring and constant pressure on the lecturers and professors to maintain a high level of quality scholarship by the publishing of significant papers in respected journals and by their attendance at prestigious conferences. In short, the American private school stresses, in addition to its social exclusivity, the importance of scholarly achievement by its faculty as a strategic factor in its success.

Academics fortunate enough to be able to work in such an environment, or indeed its rare equivalent outside the USA, are free to pursue research usually with some non-too-onerous teaching duties, whose burden may be lightened by the support of teaching assistants, part-timers recruited from the brighter and more ambitious graduate students. Faculty are relatively free of financial problems and they may even be able to supplement their academic salaries with additional private consultancy. Indeed, in some schools, a teacher who was not able to earn a substantial additional external income would not be employable because of doubts about his standing in his profession.

In that productive atmosphere scholastic activity flourishes. The payback to the employing school is not only prestige and recognition because those places are not philanthropies. Quite the opposite, they are built on sound business commonsense. What the university gets in return is a steady stream of patents, inventions and income-generating, lucrative cooperations with successful corporations. There is no shortage of wealthy businessmen willing to pay top dollar for access to the talents of the best brains, not to say the kudos of being associated with a leading academic brand name. This is why the best high-tech companies flock to set up their stalls around top university campuses.

The American private university system works well and keeps the prestigious Ivy League universities and other top schools in the top of the league of world universities mainly because the best universities have a sense of the long-term. They are no less businesses than any other commercial operation where customers buy a service at the market price. But they are not run for short-term profit. Most importantly, they understand that, in the academic trade, it is quality which sells. The finances of the top institutions are tied up in trusts and their operating profits are returned to improve the quality and added-value of the academic product on offer.

Regulation of the financial affairs of such a school will be overseen by a board of regents or trustees, usually consisting of the some of the great and the good in whose, always financially disinterested, hands would lie the responsibility for maintaining the best qualities of the institution and supervising the most prudent use of its assets.

That, at least, is what I had always understood when I was told that I would be working for a private university. Unfortunately, the American Institute of Cyrpus was 'private' only in the sense that it had a single businessman-owner who called himself 'Chancellor'. I do not doubt that the owner/chancellor often had visions of himself as a public benefactor when he first decided to expand his business empire to take in the education trade and build himself a private university. University education is a lucrative business in Northern Cyprus. The TRNC, with a population smaller than that of Croydon, could boast no less than six private universities-and all of them were making big money from the surplus of would-be students from the Turkish mainland.

The opportunity was there. Turkey had had a population explosion in the 1970's and 1980's and did not build enough institutions of higher education in time for those children to grow to university age. So Northern Cyprus currently takes anything up to fifty thousand of this surplus and even more provision is being planned. These students are not usually the first-cut, as it were. More likely, they have not been able to find a university place in Turkey and therefore have had to be shipped off to Cyprus. But they will always be welcome at AIC, which will accept any potential student who can find his or her way to the tuition cashier's desk without a map.

It is probably a win-win situation. The Turkish parents can boast that they have children at college while not having them hanging around the house for a few years. The Turkish government sees a relief valve for its burgeoning student-age population and overcrowded schools. The students themselves, not being especially gifted academically, can attend a university where they will not be intellectually over-stressed. And the owner/chancellor will make a good few quid (or euros, or dollars or YTL or any other reliable convertible currency).

The students do particularly well out of the deal. If they had stayed in Istanbul or Ankara, their options would be limited. They might find themselves unemployed, or worse, made to learn the restaurant trade as a waiter or waitress in the family business while Mama plans a fast marriage. The only hope of freedom for the men would be the year's conscription in the army. On the other hand, being a pretend student in Cyprus gives them years of liberty. Unlimited if they arrange their course failures creatively. For a libidinous twenty-year-old, a horizonless future of sex and idleness is definitely preferable to the suffocating alternative.

So 'private' TRNC universities were born. The owner/chancellor saw his chance and took it. After all, he had a long provenance as a successful business man. Not of course, in anything as conventional as education but one business is pretty much like another, is it not? He started his business life, as far as anyone could tell, as a maker and seller of luxury goods—Louis Vutton, Burbery, Versache and Dulce Gabbana for example. It is not recorded whether he would also sell genuine certificates of authenticity as well.

Then there were the perfumes. Real Parisian scents—Channel, Max Facter, Yves St. Lorent. His cake shops (sorry, "patisseries") also went very well. All across the country his name could be seen emblazoned on shops in most of the towns and villages. Then there were the travel agencies and the insurance company. Add to that the motor-cycle franchise and the car show-room. So, with all this wealth of business experience, what was more natural than moving into the higher education trade?

Ah, I hear you say, even in a country like North Cyprus, one can't just put up a sign and start selling degrees. You have to get permission, provide a long-term plan, demonstrate academic experience, put down financial guarantees. What about YODAK—the Northern Cyprus Ministry of Education? Don't you have to get a licence from them?

Well, yes, all that is true, but to quote that oft-heard phrase, "This is Cyprus". Inflexible rules which would stop the project dead in any other country, such as the requirement of British universities to obtain a royal charter, certainly do exist in Northern Cyprus. It is just that Cypriot rules, in any walk of life, are not absolute definitions of what must and must not be done. They are more like suggestions or guidelines which may be applied rigidly or ignored completely depending on the situation and the people involved. The subtlety of their application is dependent on so many factors—social, familial, political, favours owed, how important is the person seeking a favour and so on. It has even been rumoured that, in a society owned and managed by an oligarchy of corrupt politicians and international criminals, money does occasionally change hands, shock horror!

So, getting oneself one's own university is probably a piece of cake (Sorry, patisserie!), for the well-connected car-salesman. Borrow a couple of million, throw up a couple of buildings ("My brother he has ver' ver' good construction company."), appoint a few senior staff from your home village and build a faculty from civil service retirees. Then it's just a matter of waiting for thousands of innocent young faces to get off the Izmir-Kyrenia ferry clutching shedloads of lovely euros.

Running a traditional business such as a car showroom or supermarket is mainly a matter of deciding on an appropriate business strategy and applying various business processes to make it work. All the previous experience of the owner/chancellor had been in running businesses with cost-led business strategies. Perfumes and handbags with designer names are for sale all over the island and there is a used car lot on every street corner. So to stay in business, the handbag faker or second-hand car dealer must sell on price.

Unfortunately, these cost-led business strategies will not work when it comes to higher education. The most appropriate business strategy, that of differentiating the product by quality, is not available at short notice—Oxford and The Sorbonne have had 800 years to reach the front. So to meet his profit margins, the owner had to resort to quicker methods, which amounted to stuffing in as many students as could be accommodated and charge them as much as he could get away with.

To maximise margins, everything else-books, teachers, computers, staff salaries, even classroom aids like projectors-was considered a cost or an overhead to be minimised. Faculty were very badly paid—a top of the scale senior professor would be paid about €25,000 a year, a senior lecturer would earn as little as €12,000. There were no wasteful faculty benefits—no holiday pay, no pension plan, no sick pay unless approved (i.e. your salary would be docked if your sickness was short-term or not serious enough), no maternity leave, no health insurance. No-one could live on the wages in what is a very expensive country, so the locals who worked at the AIC were either supplementing their pensions, like me, or were women bringing in a little extra to the family budget.

Sometimes an Institute job was a supplement to some other business on the local economy. For example, the Head of Tourism was also a successful restaurateur. When he was fired, it was generally agreed that one could not easily combine the roles of full-time senior professor and running one of the TRNC's more successful eateries.

Classes at the Institute were far too long at 3 hours but the length did make for easy time-tabling. It is very difficult to do proper justice to a lecture if it is longer than one hour. After about 45-50 minutes, the human attention span comes to an end. What I did in my lectures was to give a 15 minute break every hour but even that did not stop my students mentally drifting off to another planet towards the end of the three hours.

Those students who did actually stay, of course. Which was usually less than half of them. A class of 70 students would be signed up for, say, systems analysis or software engineering, two subjects which need, for their understanding, some degree of attention. With seventy students paid-up, one could look forward to a class attendance of maybe forty, the rest relying on the famous Cypriot examination techniques and their personal support networks. The first to leave would be departing after about ten minutes and there would be a steady exodus thereafter until the final class attendance would be reduced to a hard core of fifteen or so. If questioned why they were sloping off while the teacher was talking, they would cite their need for a smoke break, as if it were a basic civil right. Who could argue, given the personal smell of some of them, that they were at the mercy of a serious addiction which needed regular feeding and which would, in due course, require serious medical attention?

The absence of paper-based textbooks meant that the Institute could claim to be in the forefront of educational innovation with its boasts that it was a 'paperless' institution, a crusading electronic pioneer of all things modern, efficient and up-to-date. If so, then one would have expected something approaching state-of-the-art electronic systems. But the Institute's computer network was basic, with regular breakdowns. It was glacially slow, probably because of its being based on the region's cheapest Internet Service Provider in Beirut. I complained to the IT Director repeatedly. Without effect, of course. After a visit to IT, I sometimes heard their laughter after they had fobbed me off.

So why did the workforce put up with these demonic conditions? Salaries could have been raised to fair international levels which would have improved faculty morale and made staff retention easier. Money could have been spent on infrastructure and facilities. It would appear that the money should have been there. After all, 5-6,000 students each year, each bringing at least €4,000 plus extras means an annual income in excess of twenty million euros. Subtract faculty salaries—say 200 full-time equivalents on an average of, let us say, €15,000 pa-would only cost about three million. There would be support staff and utilities and other things to pay for but one would have thought that there would be plenty of income to meet all expenditures and still leave a tidy profit. It seems not-the Institute was rife with rumours about unpaid elecricity bills and demands for back taxes.

For all the wide difference between income and expenditure, the Institute appeared to be in continuous financial difficulties. During my year and a half there, I witnessed several purges when staff and faculty were fired—without notice or final salary, naturally. Those are the business processes of the supermarket—pile 'em high and sell 'em cheap. Or, actually not so cheap. In the academic year 2008-2009 there was a 20% increase in student numbers and a 10% increase in tuition fees. A sneak look at the AIC business plan showed that revenues for the next year would be expected to be over €30million. More and more students and fewer and fewer professors to teach them! What a brilliant way to make money!! If the owner/chancellor could only get rid of the few remaining teachers, sell off all the buildings and reduce the administration just to taking in student fees, then he could keep all those euro millions for himself!!

Six

It was now November and we had been in the TRNC for two months. Because of the penny-pinching way salaries were paid, this was the first month when I had received full salary. We had been living on my British pensions and some savings but money had been leaking away fast. Living costs were much higher than we expected them to be—easily as high as in the UK. We would spend just about the same at the local Astro supermarket as we would spend at Tecso's in England for food that was significantly inferior in choice and quality. The other basic living costs-electricity, water, transport and so on were not much different than what we would have paid in London or Paris. In addition to the expenses of everyday living, we also had the outgoings needed to pay for the privilege of working at AIC-the costs of getting immigration papers, the blood tests—as well as the deposits for the supply of electricity and water.

There was also the £800 deposit for the apartment which, technically, was supposed to be refundable. But, as other expatriate faculty pointed out to us, 'refundable deposit' has no direct Turkish translation—once the money had been paid over, it had become the personal property of the landlord. However carefully the tenant had looked after the property, the landlord would never accept any responsibility for returning the deposit. Nor indeed, we were sure, would Ozalay feel that he would be, as we say in

England, 'pulling a fast one' i.e. acting dishonestly, in keeping our money. We were foreigners and therefore we should have no expectation that he had any obligation to us to treat us fairly. More likely, if we were to ask for our money back, he would almost certainly feel offended that we would be insulting him by trying to cheat him out of his well-deserved deposit.

This relentless cash haemorrhage was fed by regular visits to the cashpoints to raid our savings account in France and my old-age pension in England. The ATM was another hazard.

The ATM's did not always work. Sometimes they would be able to connect to our French account and sometimes to our British accounts and sometimes to neither—the card would be rejected before a transaction could be commenced. This was not a serious problem because all the various banks' ATM's were independent of each other. Local banks in the TRNC do not have any interconnection so if you get a bank debit card from one bank, it will only work at that bank's hole-in-the-wall. If your bank was located in the town centre, that meant a long walk. Unless, of course, you had international cards like us. When the ATM's were working, international cards were acceptable at most machines, since they provide a source of hard currency to the local economy. There were times when an ATM transaction would go through almost to completion save for delivering the money. The ATM gave no indication that the aborted transaction had been rolled back so it was always important to save the printed receipt and then use the Internet at the Institute or at a cybercafe to check that money had not been debited from our accounts. I don't think I was ever seriously cheated but in the highly-stressful environment we found ourselves in, it is quite possible that I had donated the odd hundred pounds or so to the Turkish Cypriot economy or to one of its banks.

As soon as I started to get paid, I opened a euro account at the bank from which the Institute paid our salaries which fell due at the first of the month when we got the third of the YTL salary for the month in arrears and on the fifteenth of the month when the remaining two-thirds of the salary was paid in euros. This bank, called The Iktisat Bank, had a foreign department where expatriates could deal with helpful staff in English. We soon became friendly with one of the staff there. She was, like many locals, originally from Cyprus but familiar with the English way of life after having spent much of her life in the UK.

By the beginning of November I had been paid half of one month's salary during October and I was waiting for another tranche of money at the beginning of November. It was, as so often, as soon proved customary, late. I still had a few Euros left from mid-October in my salary account and I withdrew those in pounds. Then I withdrew YTL from my UK account at an ATM and assembled the rent money after changing the YTL at a money-changer, who gave me, not unexpectedly, a ruinous rate of exchange. I got back to the apartment just in time to meet Ozalay, who had already slithered around for his rent in 'sterling pounds'.

Our routine was now established. I would go into the office about lunchtime and work from about 1.00pm until 9.00pm when my evening graduate classes came to an end. These were held on Tuesday, Wednesday and Friday evenings which meant that I would take a taxi there and get the Institute's shuttle bus back, which would stop near the Astro supermarket. Weekdays I would get home to a light meal cooked by Loydz although on Fridays we would usually meet up at the CafeDaD for a couple of glasses of wine first. It was a comfortable routine for the most part.

Ozalay decided that we would need a car.

"My brother. He has car. Ver' cheap. Good to run."

But we decided that, given we were not intending to stay in TRNC for ever, and, what is more, we soon realised that owning a car in Kyrenia would inevitably involve extortionate insurance as well as multiple trips to the police station and/or Lefkosa to complete the elaborate, and expensive, bureaucratic formalities which are unavoidable for foreigners to Northern Cyprus who want their own wheels. We did come across the occasional expatriate with a car but a few enquiries soon established that cars were a major headache to own, run and pay for. Given that Kyrenia is such a small place, taxis were numerous, and while they were not cheap, they were reliable. Northern Cyprus is only about the size of a largish English county and has few roads, so it was difficult to make a case for paying through the nose for a car unless one had special reasons such as the need to take children to school or because one had chosen to live a long way from town. For us, taxis would do nicely. The shuttle bus was also useful. It went hourly to and from the campus, stopping quite near the apartment. We only ever used it to ride home—trips into the Institute were by taxi. The last nightly bus left the campus at 9.00 pm when we would even be able to get a seat. If Loydz had come to my class, as she usually did, then seats on the bus were usually made available for the professor and his lady—one of the more attractive qualities of the students being a respect for gender, age and seniority, long since vanished from England. So I ended my class at five to nine and got the bus. Before that I had to sign the room key back in. This was done by the honour system. I just signed the book and hung up the key in the cupboard. I think there was supposed to be a security man on duty but I only ever saw him once. He addressed me in Turkish.

"Have you locked the room?"

"Yes, it's locked", I told him in English.

"Have you signed the book?" in Turkish.

"Yes, and I have hung up the key", in English.

'Thank you. Good night", again in Turkish.

"Goodnight." I replied.

Well, how come my sudden fluency in this foreign language? Actually, I have been teaching evening school since 1967 and I have had this conversation a hundred times in several languages. What else could he have been saying?

Apart from my weekly unequal struggle with the Friday undergraduate statistics class, my classes were not difficult to teach. Actually the statistics would not have been difficult either but it is difficult to explain the subtleties of say, Bayes Theorem, against a roaring gale of Turkish cross-talk and the constant comings and goings of the students. But the other classes with between 10 and 20 students per class were what I was used to and I had full sets of course material. For the programming class there was sufficient technology at the Institute that I could prepare on my laptop and deliver the class interactively via overhead projector. Database and MIS classes subjects I had been teaching for at least fifteen years at my previous colleges and it was not difficult to edit my notes for photocopying so that the class had hard-copy material to guide them. By this means, I was able to keep a clear conscience over the matter of photocopying: I was merely recycling my own stuff which I had been accumulating since I first started teaching those subjects in the 1980's.

That is not to say that I was delivering a history course on the subject. Newer aspects of the courses, which had entered the syllabus in the last five years or so and on which I was not entirely expert, such as the Internet languages UML and XBRL involved my having to do some private study. But updating one's personal skills base is meat and drink for an academic and I did my best to present the smart young men and women from Iran and beyond with the very latest of information.

My relations with TFC changed subtly. She came to realise that I did not exactly respect her learning, or rather its lack thereof, when it came to the academic subject matter of the department. It is true to say that I made it very clear that I considered her to be deficient in relevant subject expertise and I would hit back every time she attempted to bully me with her shows of anger. But she would not entirely give up and she would still barge into my office from time to time to demand I drop everything and go to her office where she would make some oblique reference to my insolence and demand that I complete the task of rewriting all my lecture notes for her project to create an online graduate MIS course, something which I had absolutely no intention of doing. Even without my involvement, I could be sure it would come to nothing.

Her attempts to challenge me directly were futile since I took little or no notice of her. She interpreted this as arrogance on my part but under her bluster, I could sense that she was afraid of me. So she had to resort to more underhand ways to attack. Since she was now handling the administration of the graduate program, she took it upon herself to begin some of the program redesign. She started by deciding to remove a couple of courses in mainstream MIS and to create a new course in research methods. Naturally this was not what was needed and I told her so, copying my memo to the Dean of Graduate Studies and to the Rector. As a result, the program changes were put on hold, much to her annoyance. Later on, when I had gained management control of the program, I was able to reorganise the course curriculum to something which was both up-to-date and relevant.

Another little trick she played was to devise a student evaluation form which was only presented to my classes and not to anyone else's. Reban was instructed to administer this test to my students. The questions were cleverly phrased e.g. 'How well do you understand the way the professor speaks?' or 'Do you find the professor easy to follow?' Given that a quarter of the class were monoglot Turkish, half had little better than tourist English and that only 25% of them could be considered anything like fluent in the language of instruction, it is not surprising what answers she was expecting. I never got to see the results or hear any more about them.

Then there was the time-table trick when, as head of department, she was asked to report on room allocations by the Institute's Provost. Naturally, her report did not include my classes which meant, had it gone through, that my students would have had to meet in the corridor or under the trees in the campus square. Fortunately, the Provost, no friend of hers, spotted her deliberate omission and put things right. I liked the Provost, a very decent sixty-something Russian-Jewish intellectual whose wife worked for AIC as a professor of education. She had been seriously ill but was still working as a head of department. The Provost was not fired during the next purge. No, his wife was. Some said that she had been fired to make a safe berth for TFC herself. The upshot was that the Provost could not possibly continue to work there under such humiliating circumstances and he resigned as well.

It was clearly time for another meeting with the Rector to complain and ask for a transfer to another department such as computer science, where there was a shortage of people to teach my subjects. He heard me out and then just told me to get on with my teaching and research and not to involve myself with any sort of administration. I had considered the Rector to be a rather civilised old gentleman but clearly he did not have the power to confront the destructive force that was TFC. Why, I wondered? Maybe she really did have political power beyond anyone else in the. One of the office women had overheard my complaints

"Don't bother", she said, "students and teachers come into his office every day with complaints about her. He has a stack of student complaints but nothing can be done."

So, I was relieved of my administration. Since my teaching was completely taken care of and presented little in the way of preparation, I set down to concentrate on research.

Or I would have done, had I not been hit by the completely unexpected. I suddenly needed urgent medical care for a condition I had not been aware of. Fortunately, it happened over a weekend. Had it happened during an evening class I would have been in serious trouble. During the evening, my class was often the only class in the building. There was no telephone and the security guards were usually notable by their absence. Later, when I had recovered, I was always accompanied to evening classes by Loydz so that if I were to fall ill again, she would be able to summon an ambulance.

We had noticed a small private clinic about a quarter of a mile from our apartment and on Sunday afternoon, we approached them with my emergency. The clinic was almost empty but the resident physician, a gynaecologist by profession, took me in and found me a bed in a room with a cot for Loydz. Since we were obviously going to stay the night, she immediately went back to pack a bag. The consultant who would be treating me, the smart young Doctor Necmi, arrived later that evening. He immediately diagnosed a problem requiring immediate surgery. After an uncomfortable night, I was, the following morning, X-rayed and given an ultrasound examination. Then I was told 'nil by mouth' and driven by ambulance from Kyrenia to a small private hospital in Famagusta where there was a suitable operating theatre and the right equipment.

Later that Monday evening I had a general anaesthetic and my condition was stabilised. They then let me rest for a few days until the

Friday when I was able to have the necessary operation to cure me. During this time Loydz stayed in my room and we dined together on hospital food. The nurses and Doctor Necmi were first class. My vital signs were taken round the clock and I was regularly admonished by the nursing staff to drink 'very, very water'. The care I got was excellent and after a night's sleep following the operation, I was fit to go home. It had taken just one week.

If getting first-class hospital care had been accomplished without problem, paying for it was another matter altogether. When the bill was presented, for a very reasonable four thousand euros, I did what I had done at the Kyrenia clinic and pulled out my credit card.

"Is not possible," said the young woman on reception whose job it was to issue invoices and collect payments.

"Why not?"

"My machine for credit card. She is broken."

"I have several cards. Maybe one of the others?"

"Not possible. All broken."

"I will write you a cheque in euros drawn on my French account."

"No, that is not possible. We not accept cheques."

"What shall I do?"

"You must pay by credit card or cash."

"I can't pay cash because I don't have that amount of cash with me. And I can't go to the ATM because the daily limit is only YTL 500."

"You have big problem. Maybe you come back tomorrow when my machine will be good."

"I have just had surgery and I need to rest. Besides I have no car. It will take me all day to travel to and from Famagusta from Kyrenia."

"This is very bad."

This game of ping-pong went on for a few more exchanges until she reluctantly agreed to accept a cheque drawn on a French bank, while making it abundantly clear that I was making life unnecessarily difficult for her.

It was now Saturday afternoon and I was still dopey from the anaesthetic. Apparently my operation had taken over three hours. So I was looking forward to enjoying two or three days convalescence before I went back to work for my Tuesday evening class. The Institute was quite sympathetic to my plight and while in hospital I had received a very sympathetic phone call from the Rector. Also Tugce, the young woman who was half student/half employee and who had been the first to greet us when we had arrived at Ercan airport, also paid me a visit, bringing some biscuits and fruit. It was a very kind gesture to travel all that way. I also got a kind message from Reban who had been holding the MIS fort in my week's absence.

My short convalescence was interrupted by a necessary visit to the Iktisat Bank to talk to the very nice Anglo-Cypriot lady who had now become our friend. I explained the problem of paying for my medical care and how the accounts people at the Famagusta hospital had awarded me the problem of their broken credit card reader.

"Well," she began, "you could go back to Famagusta which will take about four hours and cost you about 150 YTL."

I didn't like the sound of that.

"Or you could get the money in cash and get a taxi driver to deliver it."

I liked that even less.

"Or you could do what a lot of local people do and that is to give your card to the driver. Which will also cost you 150 YTL for him to go there."

It was getting worse so I asked her why the cheque option was so bad.

"Well, the main problem is that most banks in this country do not have cheque clearing facilities with banks in the European Union."

"But", she said, "I will see what I can do."

Over the next six weeks there were frantic phone calls between me, the Iktisat Bank and Famagusta to try to get this massive problem solved. Eventually, the nice lady from The Iktisat phoned to tell me of the success. She had managed to get the cheque cleared somehow and my debt to the Famagusta hospital had been settled. Naturally such things do not come cheap when I found that a hundred euros had been debited from my account for bank charges.

When I got back to the Institute after my week in hospital, I went first to Human Resources to ask if they had any sort of insurance scheme for faculty who suddenly found themselves hospitalised. I could swear that the Human Resources Director was stifling a laugh.

"No, I"m sorry, we don't do anything like that." she said with the sort of pitying smile she might have given me had I invited her to an orgy.

"In fact, you don't even qualify for commercial health insurance", she went on, "there is no insurance for the over 65's."

"What? Those are the people who need it most! What are they supposed to do? Die on cue?"

"If their families can't help them, then they have to go public. There is a basic health service of sorts."

I could imagine what that would be like.

"You have been away for a week so you will need to let me have your absence report. A medical certificate will do."

"I won't have that until I see the surgeon for the follow-up consultation in a couple of weeks."

'That's fine", she said, "according to AIC regulations, you are supposed to give it to your line manager."

TFC!! Give my medical details to TFC!! That was certainly not going to happen.

But it did not stop TFC from asking me for it every other day for the next month. When I next met Dr. Necmi, and I got the full report of the procedures I had undergone during my week in hospital, I copied it and gave the photocopy directly to Human Resources with a warning that it was confidential. The next time I was questioned by TFC, I was pleased to be able to tell her that the matter was closed.

With no administration by order of the Rector, I was at something of a loose end. Just do teaching and research he had said. I hadn't done much research for several years. My experience of research is that if you are not in a top university where scholarship is taken seriously, then research is the surest way to stay unpromoted. In most British universities except the top twenty or so older universities, it is most unusual for someone to advance their careers by a prolific publications record. Most promotions are awarded for doing so-called 'administration'. Lip-service is paid to research and 'bringing in money' for research contracts but neither teaching nor research will be taken into account at a promotion interview compared with a record of service on the equal opportunities committee or for writing, say, an unreadable report on student exchanges. The quickest way to the top in the average middle—or lower-ranking British university is to pack your CV with this sort of unscholastic clerical make-work. It will look good at interviews on the promotion chase because it will be read by interviewers who had come up the academic greasy pole by precisely the same route. It was certainly going to be the same in Kyrenia. Suggesting I do research was little more than a crude way to sideline me.

The Rector was certainly aware of the depth of ill-feeling between TFC and me: she had been to his office often enough to complain about my insolence and disobedience and, given her political connections, she would probably have easily been able get me dismissed. I often wondered why I was kept on, unless it was because I was needed for window dressing for the upcoming accreditation exercise when the Institute would be seeking a new five-year licence to sell its degrees. For this to go through, it needed international faculty with doctoral degrees. Thus I figured I would be safe for at least eighteen months until after the state visit from the Cyprus and Turkish ministries of education, the day after which I would be unceremoniously thrown out.

But nevertheless, I started some research projects, mainly to fill the time, not having career advancement to worry about. Sometimes it is quite comforting when one has a brilliant, or, in my case, modest, career behind one. So, relieved of any responsibility for administering the graduate program, I started to think about how I would fill my time with some academic, or at least quasi-academic, creative endeavour.

About this time, I was called to a meeting, over lunch, with some of the Institute's top people including the Director of International Affairs. Also at the meeting were senior faculty from the Department of Computer Engineering and the usual ragbag of managers and hangers-on who always appear at academic meetings when a free lunch is on offer. Whatever could it be about, I wondered? The International Director showed us a newspaper article from *The International Herald Tribune* on the subject of quad-core microprocessors—*Quad-core computing. The hot issue—what will the next generation of computer chips be like?*

The problem, briefly, is that the methods for computer chip design which have worked spectacularly well for nearly forty years, can't really, for a variety of technical reasons, be pushed much further. It is not possible to increase the number of micro-switches on the silicon chip much beyond the present limit—further miniaturization is out of the question. So current thinking is to make the next generation of microprocessors simpler but with more of them, four to be exact, working in parallel on the same chip. The big industry players are working to find a way to make this work. Thousands of the best and best-paid computer—and software engineers at companies like Microsoft, Intel, Samsung, AMD *et al.* are working on the problem.

"Can we get involved?" the ID asked us, "Maybe we can get into this?"

I tried to explain the scale of the problem—his idea was not far from the equivalent of suggesting that AIC develop a space program in competition to NASA. The technical people around the table nodded in agreement. I offered to write a report on the difficulties of solving the problem of managing the 'out of sequence' problem as it is called. This is when the computer instructions of the program arrive at the processors in an orderly sequence but are processed in parallel and therefore may lose their logical order. It is a problem which has baffled computer engineers for the whole of the computer age. But I wrote a report and it was published in the Institute's internal research journal.

I also wrote another article about the same time, which was also published internally, about the encryption methods of the Secure Socket Layer—the way in which data such as credit card details may be sent securely over an open phone line. The journal was loosely peer-reviewed although I did not set out to be especially original. However, each paper did contain a minimal amount of originality. That was not really the point of these publications—they were an attempt to kindle a small flame of scholarly activity in what was, almost exclusively, an establishment given over to fairly low-level teaching.

Those two articles were written fairly quickly and I moved on to another two projects which had been simmering at the back of my mind for a year or two. The first was a paper on population growth functions which was eventually published in "Mathematics Today", the bi-monthly newsletter of the Institute of Mathematics and its Applications, in August 2008. I am pleased to say it attracted a little interest including a follow-up letter in the October issue and a request from the editor of a fringe-science magazine who asked me for permission to reprint it.

At the same time, I met a fine Iranian computer scientist called Amir, who was working for peanuts teaching in the Department of Computer Engineering. Because he had only recently completed his MSc, he was still only a senior lecturer. Without a PhD, promotion to Assistant—, and later to Associate—and Full Professor was closed. So he was also working at getting his doctorate as quickly as possible. Meanwhile, as a senior lecturer, he was a dogsbody, teaching six three-hour classes a week and grading literally hundreds of assignments and examinations each term. But he was willing to lend an hour or so a week to take part in a small research group based upon his masters' dissertation which had been on the subject of text-searching. I also enrolled another graduate student, Abbasabadi, also Iranian, who had been a professional software engineer in Teheran. We began a series of seminars and discussion groups and software development for probablistic text searching.

This heretical behaviour of mine did not go unnoticed by TFC. As head of department, she felt that she should be the director of any departmental research effort. What she then did was to call Amir and Abbasabadi into her office and asked them to do research for her instead with me. I am pleased to say that both of them rejected her kind offer.

It was around that time, just before Christmas 2008, that TFC came banging into the office to present Reban and me with our assignments for the following term. This time I was to be given the undergraduate fourth-year course in operating systems in addition to my three graduate classes. She also told me that no PhD courses would be offered, courses which were one-on-one tutorials with some of the half dozen doctoral students. I was quite happy about operating systems, a subject I have taught many times. Clearly she did not want the course for herself-I had noticed, on her table, a copy of the classic *Operating Systems* by Andrew Tannenbaum, the standard work on the subject. It was still in its pristine virginal condition, having never been opened. She had obviously failed to find some mathematics course for me and realising that operating systems is too difficult to teach unless one first knows something about it, she had, no doubt reluctantly, offloaded *IS 403 Operating Systems* on to me. Before the meeting ended, she could not resist giving me another telling-off for not committing my lecture notes to her online project. I told her that the project was ill-conceived and I would not work on it unless I were able to be involved in the planning stages. I could see her blood pressure rising, so I made my excuses and left her office.

A few days later I received a memo from the Dean of Graduate Studies asking which doctoral courses I would be offering this upcoming term. He copied it with a memo from TFC outlining a couple of PhD courses which the MIS Department would be putting on. The date on her memo was the same as the date of the meeting where she had told me the exact opposite. What trick was this, I wondered? By now I was reaching the limits of my tolerance of her mental instability, her constant antagonism, her incessant sniping and these cheap tricks she was continually inventing to try to unsettle and undermine me. I went to see the Graduate Dean, an eminent German academic.

"I think she wants to do them herself", he told me.

"But I thought PhD courses could only be given by full professors, according to the Institute's regualtions?"

"Well, yes", he replied, "but I think she has the idea that if she does some doctoral courses, they will make her a full professor."

"That's a strange way of doing things. She has no real knowledge of the subject. Shouldn't she know something about state-of-the-art information systems before she becomes a full professor in the subject?"

"In most places, yes. But the normal rules don't apply here. This is Cyprus. She is very well connected."

If TFC had wanted to be just an administrative head of department, then I would have been happy to let her do it as long as I could have just got on with my academic duties. University heads of department have to do a lot of administration as well as having to dirty their hands with a lot of squalid trivial politics. I had no great wish to spend my time doing those things and had she been a head of department with sufficient self-confidence to let me teach and provide the academic leadership, it might have been possible to create a *modus vivendi* with her which would have made for a bearable working environment. But she wanted more than that, she wanted to be academic head as well, despite having no talent or experience for it.

But unfortunately, her vindictive personality problems notwithstanding, she also possessed the Turkish mentality regarding position and rank. Consensual management is a totally alien concept in Turkish culture. If you have the rank, it is your duty to give direct orders which are to be obeyed without question. If the orders are wrong or stupid, the responsibility lies not with the order-giver but with the underling who failed to carry them out properly. It is a childishly simple management philosophy.

Something had to be done and, once again, we contemplated just getting on a plane and going home to France. But Loydz had planned a visit back to her family in Manila for the following March. It seemed pointless to travel all that way west only for her to have to travel eastwards shortly after arriving in France. Leaving from Istanbul to Manila is a much shorter journey—say, only 12 or 14 hours as against maybe 36 hours from

Brittany. It was also winter and we would be getting back to a cold house in France. I still had a job which I was mostly used to doing. So having shelved the option of simply leaving, I tried one last time of several to get a transfer of department. The Rector was sympathetic-he knew TFC well-but he would not agree to my request. I needed a Plan B.

Just about this time, TFC came up with a new trick. She called all the final year MBA graduate students into her office one by one. All of them, including Abbasabadi, were well-known to me, all having attended my evening classes during the previous semester. Each was then separately threatened that if they signed up for my graduate classes, she would, as head of department, refuse to sign their applications for their graduation diplomas. When they later told me about this after classes have reconvened for the spring term in February, they were all visibly frightened.

Plan B had to be decisive. She had to be stopped. She had to be prevented from more destruction for the good of the Institute and its students. With the support of the Dean of Business and the Rector and her political connections, TFC no doubt felt herself to be totally untouchable even though, apart from those two, she had a great number of enemies. After five months of having to accept unrelenting humiliation at her hands, I also felt the need for some personal revenge. Best eaten cold, they say.

The Dean of Business and Economics, her main patron, would not be long on the payroll. He also gave graduate classes in economics. His students, from Kazakhstan, Iran and other places in central Asia, were also largely known to me, some of them having been in my introductory course in management information systems. They were all fluent in English with no Turkish. The Dean was just the opposite-entirely fluent in his native Turkish but with almost no English. Personally, I was ambivalent about his lack of English. On the one hand he could not be approached for consultation but, on the other, I was spared having to spend time listening to him. With the merest smattering of English, he was not untypical of several of the senior AIC people, even those who held to the fiction that the Institute was an anglophone institution.

One could laugh at his attempts to speak English, if one were being uncharitable. And let's face it, precious little in my Cypriot experiences so far had inclined me to charity. I bumped into the Dean of Business and Economics in the Institute square one evening when Loydz had come to meet me after class.

"How you come?" he asked her.

No, not a sexual proposition. He was merely enquiring about how she had travelled to the island.

On Christmas Day, Loydz went off to her church and I prepared roast chicken and apple sauce as per British tradition. I did try Yorkshire pudding as well, but the cooker's eccentric heating controls defeated me. Loydz had never had apple sauce before and it rapidly became one of her favourites. Christmas Day was spoilt by my having to teach an evening class whose attendance was reduced by the absence of the substantial proportion of Nigerian Christian students. It felt strange to be working. The only other time I had spent the festival in a state other than dawn-to-dusk hedonistic pleasure was when, as a teenager, I had played trombone for the Chadderton and District Silver Prize Band in Manchester, which traditionally spent Christmas morning playing carols in the streets for pennies.

Seven

No organisation is a simple power structure as depicted in those hierarchy charts much loved by management consultants. Most organisations, and especially most universities, have multiple threads of power to go with the labyrinthine politics. Indeed, in all universities, politics flourish like weeds because academics do not, in general, have jobs which consume great amounts of time or energy. They also mostly have a high opinion of their intellects and an inflated view of their social importance. Consequently they spend a lot of time doing politics. Possibly only the old Soviet Kremlin or the Vatican have politics remotely approaching, for vanity and bitterness, the politics inside a university. Henry Kissinger, who knows something about politics, doubtless found it easier to negotiate nuclear weapons with Leonid Brezhnev than to chair the Harvard University Inter-Departmental Paper Clip Allocation Committee. He got it spot on when he famously said that the reason why academic politics are so bitter is because the stakes are so low.

For all the importance the Institute attached to making itself into a cosmopolitan institution, the Turkish and Turkish Cypriots tended not to intermix too freely with the 'internationals', as the non-Turkish faculty were known. Similarly, the internationals tended to drift towards each other. The two groups were nominally integrated but in practice the two groups were too different for complete mixing. It was generally understood that while the local people were, by virtue of the status of the TRNC, virtual prisoners on the island and therefore more or less permanent until they were fired, the internationals were only transients passing through. Few lasted more than a year, some much less, before the stresses of the TRNC and the frustrations of the Institute, wore them down.

The internationals were in no doubt as to why they were there. They were necessary to the business plan of the Institute in its attempts to inject the subject expertise vital for accreditation and credibility. The intellectual gene pool of Northern Cyprus, which has a population of less than 300,000, is just too small to provide a ready supply of plausible academic expertise for all the local universities in competition for it. There was no doubt that many, but certainly not all, of the locals were resentful of the internationals. The internationals were better paid and were also free to travel, which Turkish Cypriots could only do after a long bureaucratic struggle to meet the most exacting visa and immigration restrictions. The furthest most of them would ever go would be to mainland Turkey.

But right now, travel was not uppermost in my mind-the immediate problem was what to do about TFC. So far, in my dealings with her, I had taken all the blows. I could have responded in kind and simply confronted her and shouted her down every time she tried to pull one of her tricks. But something inside told me to wait and to cultivate the Institute's several alternative power structures.

I have often found that the old adage 'what goes around comes around' contains a kernel of peasant truth. I felt an inner confidence that the battle with TFC would, sooner or later, go my way. Not least because, I realised, her aggression towards me was because she actually feared me, for some reason. And even though she would appear to hold all the cards, I had been very careful not once to let my guard down. By the first week in January 2008, shortly after Loydz and I had made the decision to stay a little longer, an opportunity to hit back presented itself. The Dean of Graduate Studies convened a meeting of the Executive Graduate Studies Council and he invited me to present a report on behalf of the MIS graduate program.

I sensed that the right moment had arrived. TFC and her Dean-Protector were also invited, possibly because the Graduate Dean was also looking forward to a public showdown as well. Other attendees also included a number of senior Deans and Professors, men of influence in the small world of the AIC and few of them supporters of the The Fat Chemist. I carefully prepared a written statement for distribution which I would read out. It was as unemotional as I could make it. I described the incident when she had blackballed the PhD student, I described how she had taken over the administration of the graduate courses in spite of what had been written on my job description and I explained her incompetent efforts to revise the graduate curriculum.

I made it clear from the outset that I would be prepared to be cross-examined on the statement and that if the matter of responsibility for the MIS graduate program were not resolved, I would resign from the Institute that very day. My statement was also a catalogue of all the slights and offences I had been made to endure since starting work in MIS the previous September. I told the Council that I had several times asked for a transfer to another department but nothing had been done. This, I pointed out, must mean that the management was quite happy with the situation and was happy to put up with a dysfunctional MIS Department

After I had read my statement, there was the expected and, I have to say, planned for, reaction.

"I AM NOT ON TRIAL!!!" bellowed TFC.

"I AM NOT ON TRIAL!!!"

In her anger, which I now realised was almost her entire emotional range, she stood up, stamped her foot a few times and took her dramatic exit, dragging the poor Dean, her patron, along behind her.

"I am not on trial!!" could be heard echoing down the corridor.

Before running after her, the Dean stopped for a few words of broken English with me.

"You move. New department. I move you. You now Department Economics."

Even more happily, TFC never spoke to me again and my life was all the richer for it. I have no doubt that she considered herself the injured party and in her quiet moments moderated her anger and resentment with liberal dashings of self-pity. But her vindictiveness continued. I did hear on the grapevine that she had refused to let student societies invite me to address them and that she had threatened some of my graduate students a second time that she would not sign their diploma applications if they were to join any of my classes.

So I became, for six months at least, a professor of economics. My new head, Ergin, was kindness and friendliness itself and I was allowed to get on with scholarly things undisturbed. During that six months I published my papers, ran my small research group for information retrieval and concentrated on what I have always considered to be the *amour propre* of the professional academic i.e. knowledge and its dissemination, without needing to confront daily that self-indulgent, self-important politicking which is the standard displacement activity of the failed university teacher.

TFC, the Dean and the Rector were all, later that year, swept away by the new broom of the incoming Rector, brought in that summer to clean up the cronyism and mutual back-scratching of the old AIC regime and to prepare the Institute for a new coat of academic respectability to parade before the educational ministries in Lefkosa and Ankara, who were gearing up for an accreditation visit against a background of the AIC's plummeting reputation. This culling took place without my knowledge, or that of anyone else I was on regular gossiping terms with. There was an external political dimension in the form of a national election which impinged on the parochial squabbling of the Institute but as an outsider, it was difficult to make out which changes were imposed by the powers-that-be in Ankara and which were the whims of the owner/chancellor.

It might be thought that I am here grinding a personal axe against TFC, that the differences between us were no more than differences of personality and attitude. My account might appear to be unnecessarily harsh and hyperbolic. To which I would say that, if anything, I erred on the side of generosity towards her. I did not dwell on her attitude to students to whom she was unfailingly unsympathetic and unhelpful. I did not mention details of the very many small acts of spite and malice to all and sundry which helped fill her day. I did not mention that she had made enemies of almost everyone she had had to work with. I did not mention the dozens of student complaints about her which I had impotently to listen to. Or the regular complaints about her to the AIC senior management.

The number of people who came up to shake my hand after I had finally stood up to her at the Graduate Council meeting, was considerable. For several days, people I had never seen before, both Turkish and international, would stop me in the corridor to smile at me and slap me on the back. Not a single person criticised what I had done. Everyone who spoke to me about it, from secretaries to vice-chancellors, congratulated me on my stand.

When I had done something wrong as a child, my mother would accuse me of 'badness' i.e. motiveless, pointless malice. In less secular times, the notion of good and evil as identifiable entities was a commonly accepted belief. It has been discarded in modern times in favour of a more causal, existential view of human beings as being freewill individuals responsible for their own behaviour. But meeting someone like TFC, and she is only the second or third individual of the type I have met in my life, one's faith in such scientific rationality is seriously tested. She was a very personification of my mother's notion of 'badness'. I never once heard her say a good thing about anyone or anything. Apart from self-pity, the only emotion she ever displayed was a corrosive, malevolent anger. She never helped anyone I knew of, she spread rumours about people and slandered them in their absence. She did not have, as far as I could see, a single redeeming crumb of humanity.

She certainly has no right to be teaching my subject in a university-level institution or to her absurd pretensions that she was possessed of outstandingly special intellectual gifts. It was indeed a good day when, later that year, she was finally removed from doing further damage to the impressionable minds of the young.

Meanwhile back home, our tenancy in Mr Ozalay's apartment was not the happiest imaginable and when we told people that we were paying £400 a month for it, they were surprised.

"You can rent a whole house for that", we were informed.

Maybe we are just naïve or innocent dupes of the Turkish Cypriot highly-honed skill at fleecing the expatriates. We had plenty of opportunities to express to Ozalay our various grievances since he was a regular visitor to the apartment and would call every few days to check up on us.

Mr. Ozalay, or 'Doctor' as he liked to be called as a retired veterinarian, would turn up frequently unannounced and spend a little time telling us about his student days in Europe and the genius of his children and grandchildren. This use of courtesy titles did not work both ways, I noticed.

While he insisted on 'Doctor', he never once returned the compliment and addressed me by my academic titles, something I felt it would be bad manners to mention. He had the common look of all sixty-something Levantine men who contain corpulence just this side of obesity. He was invariably well-turned out in slacks and a buttoned cardigan, his remaining hair pomaded and fiercely brushed back in traditional style. He also wore, as so many of us of a similar age do, light-sensitive spectacles. His conversational manner was that oily style which, while seeming superficially ingratiating, is really a cover for an underlying arrogance and contempt. During these visits he would spend some time playing with the control for the air-conditioner/heater and explaining to us the complexities of its manifold operations. These tutorials, delivered as if to a mentally-defective child, would take some 15 or 20 minutes. After explaining the intricacies of switching the air-conditioner on and off, he would move the conversation on to more general topics—the intelligence of his family members, his brilliance as a veterinary surgeon, his fluency in the German language, his experience of Europe. I learnt long ago that one of the more tiresome burdens of being a senior academic is to have to listen to other people telling you how clever they, or their children, are.

A more generous man than I am would have understood Mr. Ozalay more sympathetically. His life was conducted within very limited boundaries. It was made up of domestic chores, the occasional trip to Istanbul to see his children and grandchildren and his rather restricted social life. This last consisted of afternoons spent at a local men's club nearby where retired public servants would kill time chatting and playing backgammon. But I am not a generous man when it comes to this kind of situation and we were always careful to keep the relationship at arm's length. After all, nothing contaminates the limpid honest purity of the traditional relationship between grasping landlord and resentful tenant more than overtones of personal friendship, feigned or otherwise.

We continued to disdain his persistent efforts to get us to buy a car from one of his relatives.

"But you need a car here, Mr. Payne. No buses. You will need a car. This one is very good. My cousin has looked after it very well."

But we failed to resist his attempts to introduce us to the local art market.

"My friend has a very nice gallery. I will take you there. You will see many nice pictures you will want to buy."

Which turned out to be an overpriced tourist trap selling worthless tourist tat. After these two cons had proved fruitless, he stopped trying to extract additional money from us. But the visits continued right up until the first major problem of our tenancy.

The apartment was on the first floor of a three-storey block in a little side road off the main east-west coastal highway. The neighbourhood was quiet enough for children to play in the streets. The only drawbacks were a tendency for this particular district to be first in line for power outages and for problems with the water supply and the sewerage. The electrical blackouts were regular during that first winter—for some reason, our block and two or three others nearby would find the electricity cut off while the rest of the city was still fully lit up. The power would mostly be restored within six hours or so although the Christmas blackout went on for a whole twenty-four hours throughout Boxing Day and into the day after that.

The water supply was also problematic until Mr. Ozalay explained how it worked. Water, it seems, is supplied via water mains via a meter outside the apartment. After he had arranged an account, the municipal water suppliers installed a meter and we could have water. Between the water main and the header tank on the roof, there was a large reservoir tank and a small electrical pump would lift the water from this tank to the header tank on the roof. It would then trickle down through the solar panels to a hot water tank above the ceiling. In winter this tank would be heated by an immersion heater. So, we thought, that was that—our main utility requirements were taken care of. Oh dear, if only it had been that simple.

The first major problem we encountered was the sewage disposal problem. The overflow from the septic tank had nowhere else to run but down the street. One morning, we looked out of the window to see a stream of raw sewage about a foot wide running down the gutter of the road. The smell left us in no doubt about what it was. We contacted Mr. Ozalay.

"Yes, you must arrange for the waste tank to be emptied."

"What!! In my country we have mains sewerage!"

"Not here, Mr. Payne, this is Cyprus. Here we have no canalisation. The tank must be emptied by the truck. You must be using the toilet too much."

"But there are only two of us here and the other five flats have many occcupants."

"No, Mr. Payne, you do not understand. It is your responsibility to arrange to have the tank emptied."

"Who do I talk to?"

"I will give you a phone number."

We telephoned and finally made ourselves understood to about the third person we spoke to. He had basic English and we explained the position to him.

"I come. I empty tank. It is one hunded twent' YTL"

"One hundred and twenty!!"

"Oh yes. But for all block! You get money from all block."

There were six apartments in the block so that should have been 20 YTL apiece. Two of the apartments were empty of their absentee owners and the other three were under—now, how shall I say this?—multiple occupation. The flat below had what sounded like a dozen or so students camping out and our nearest neighbours, in the apartment just across the hall, were a close-knit family of a dozen or so whose comings and goings around the clock were announced by vicious slammings of the front door every twenty minutes or so throughout the day and night.

We tried the students first. The door was opened by a student who recognised me.

"Ah AIC!!" he said.

"Yes AIC!!" I replied.

"AIC!!"

"Yes, AIC. Now what I have come about . . ."

I was answered by a torrent of Turkish which brought several other students to the door. Clearly these students had not yet completed, or even started, the foundation year course in basic English because they just looked blank when I opened my mouth. I tried again, this time pointing to the sewage stream outside the front door and made the international money sign of drawing my right index finger across my left palm. They looked at me non-plussed. So I used one of my few Turkish words as written on the twenty lira banknote.

"Yirmi, yirmi YTL!!"

"No, no yirmi!!!"

Back to English.

"But it is your shit as well!! You are responsible."

"No pay. No pay. No yirmi!!!"

And so this standoff went on until we could stand it no more.

Next a knock on the door of the noisy apartment where the conversation went pretty much the same except that the many occupants of this apartment had even fewer English language skills. People of all ages and sexes clustered around the door to see off the Englishman. Behind the throng, the sitting room of the apartment was criss-crossed with camp beds like a refugee camp.

The conversation was the same as it had been with the students.

"No yirmi!! No pay!!"

There was no response from the other three flats so we phoned Mr. Ozalay again.

'Then, Mr. Payne, you must pay."

These exchanges enlightened us to a simple set of Cypriot life rules. First, do not get involved in any sort of community cooperation. Second, never part with money to a foreigner and third, always remember that foreigners pay for everything.

There being no alternative, we called the midnight mechanics, as the Australians call them, and paid the sewage bill for the entire block. After a day or two the smell went away and, we thought, all was well.

Not so. As I was returning from the Institute one afternoon, I was stopped by a neighbour. She was, she told me in English which showed by its estuarine accent some long familiarity with the UK, concerned about the threats to the health of children playing in the street down which was flowing raw sewage. What, she demanded to know, would I be doing about it?

"But I paid to have the tank emptied only three weeks ago!"

"Well, it is back again now. You are a professor at AIC!! I am a cousin of the Rector."

I explained what had happened and she said that the tank would need re-emptying.

Once again we got on the phone to Mr. Ozalay.

"But, Mr. Payne," he explained wearily as if to a recalcitrant child, 'there is no canalisation. There is canalisation in other parts of the town but not here."

"Surely, for public health reasons, sewage removal should be a public service?"

He then tried to pin the blame for the problem on to me.

"Mr. Payne, there is no canalisation! The tank is small because the ground under the apartment is too hard and will not absorb the waste. You must not be using the toilet properly."

"There is more than one way?!"

"Mr. Payne, you are using it too much. And you must not flush toilet paper down."

"Isn't this a matter for the municipal health department at the town hall?"

"You can try that, Mr. Payne and I have a contact there. A young woman. She is my cousin, Speak very good English."

We went off to see her. We gave her the history of the problem and told her that we were renting from Mr. Ozalay.

"This is very very difficult. You must pay to have the tank emptied."

"Isn't this a public service?"

"I don't know. This is the Water Department."

'So, who do we see about it?"

"I don't know, possibly the Sewage Department or Public Health."

"Where can we find them?"

"I don't know."

"Don't water, public health and sewage work together? And you don't know where their offices are? This is only a small town!!"

"I am sorry. This is Cyprus."

We went back to the apartment with no option but to call the midnight mechanics yet again. When we got there, we found that the mains water had been cut off. The water meters had been removed, apparently by the municipal water department, the very department we had just been speaking to. Once again back to Mr. Ozalay. He came round.

"Ah yes, Mr. Payne. They have cut off the water for everybody in the block."

"I can see that. But why?"

"You are being punished."

"Punished? Why?"

"For not paying for the waste removal."

"But we did pay, Mr. Ozalay. For the whole block!!"

"Then you must pay again. And the other people in the block must also pay their share."

"But they refuse to pay!!"

"They cannot refuse. They must pay!!"

"What if they don't pay, what then?"

"Then you must pay or the water will not be reconnected. You are being punished for not paying."

The sheer dishonesty, frustration and unfairness of the situation was starting to make me seethe with anger. Indeed, I was even beginning to understand why TFC had been so angry all the time. What I was having difficulty getting my head around was why everyone living in Northern Cyprus did not live their lives in a continuous state of gut-busting fury. But no, generally people acted with a placid fatalism. 'Someone else will fix it' was the invariable attitude. The only people who ever feel any anger about this stinking situation were those interfering foreigners who go to live in Cyprus and then make an unreasonable fuss about shit and piss running down the street.

There had been a related but much bigger problem about the same time when the walls of the sewage treatment facility had collapsed and discharged tons of untreated sewage into the sea, thus putting several beaches out of use for some months. That problem too, was awarded to someone else, and so the repairs were organised and paid for by the European Union office in Nicosia. Technically, Northern Cyprus is part of the EU, even though the Northern Cypriots do not accept the EU rules and regulations. Accepting EU euros, of course, is an entirely different matter.

I could tell from the attitude of the neighbour, who had just stopped short of telling me so, that the problem, somehow, was entirely our fault. We personally were now being blamed for the sewerage overflow and the cutting off of the water. There is a certain twisted logic to what passed as reasoning in the minds of our neighbours. After all, before we had taken the tenancy, the problem had not been there. And what is more, we had been forced, quite reluctantly, into trying to get the problem solved. So, logically, we must be guilty by association.

Once again we called the boys with the tanker, who were now starting to recognise our voices over the phone. Even better, one of them could speak a little English. So when they came that evening, I asked them to speak to our neighbours to ask them to contribute to the waste-removal costs for the whole block. The ten or so students were roused and, after a great deal of bickering agreed to club together and put in thirty YTL between them.

Our noisy neighbours across the hall were also indignant at being asked for money. They too, obviously thought the entire problem was none of their business. But, much to his credit, the tanker driver, after about twenty minutes argy-bargy, did manage to convince all eight of them that yes, their waste disposal was not a free service and the costs had to be shared between all the occupants of the six apartments in the block. Eventually they stumped up another thirty, handed over with a very bad grace. The other three apartments were unoccupied, so that left only sixty for my wife and me to find as our share of the costs.

The next problem was to get the water reconnected. The water level in the ground tank was running low and would almost certainly run dry in a day or so. We were not convinced that the water department at the town hall would reconnect us with the same speed and enthusiasm they had shown in cutting us off. We consulted Ozalay yet again.

"Water? Is no problem, Mr. Payne! I have friend with water tanker. He fill your tank. I send him."

"How much does he charge?"

"He is good price! Maybe eight, ten YTL for a tonne."

"Ten YTL!! But the water department only charges one YTL!"

"But he has tanker, Mr. Payne! He deliver. Good water!"

"Let's just wait, shall we, Mr. Ozalay? I will let you know after I have spoken to the town hall"

"But his price is best in Cyprus!"

"I'll talk to you tomorrow."

Albertin, the football-mad proprietor of the CafeDaD, was a friend or kinsman, we never worked out which, of the mayor of the city who would drop into the place frequently to drink coffee with his coterie of political buddies and comely groupies. While there, His Worship would network the locals in the traditional politicianly way-an election was imminent. I later found out that he was also a close friend of my colleague Reban but then I should not have been surprised at that. In the febrile world of who-knows-who in Northern Cyprus, everyone has been to school together, or they are related to each other or they are the friend-of-a-friend or they have just slept together. In the TRNC, the degrees of separation between any two individuals would never be as large as six. The usual number would be nearer to two or fewer.

Mr. Mayor was a smartly-dressed shrewd-looking man in early middle age who carried himself with the air of someone who has the whole party machine in his pocket. We interrupted him during his flesh-pressing to tell him of the sewage problems in our street and the cutting off of the water. And he promised to do something about it.

He was as good as his word, as politicians sometimes are, especially in election year. The next day the water was reconnected and within a week or two, the diggers and excavators arrived from the municipality to begin digging the trenches and connecting Oycalsin Apartments 60, our formal address, to the mains sewerage system. The workers finished the main part of the pipe-laying and connection inside a month although the final finishing of the road surface had to wait for another three months. But the job was done, thus proving the old sayings that it's not what you know, it's who you know and it is always best to go straight to the top.

Thank you Mr. Mayor, you played a blinder. I would vote for you. If I had a vote, that is.

Spring is when Northern Cyprus is at her best. The short cool winter ends around March, which is regarded as a 'half-and-half' month-half winter and half summer. Although Cyprus never gets very cold, there are times when the tops of the thousand-metre high Kyrenian mountains get a small topping of snow. But winter in Cyprus can still be uncomfortable. The houses are uninsulated and unheated so that when the temperatures drop down below 10 °C, it is hard to remember that one left all one's warm winter clothes back in England because one would never need them in Cyprus. But with the coming of spring and sunshine, the island perks up and starts to prepare itself for another summer of heatwaves, water shortages and tourists.

My work was going well, or at least as well as it could do in the difficult working conditions. I was still cramped in half a tiny office shared with Reban and, at all times of the working day up to half a dozen students in consultation which usually meant protesting their grades noisily and vehemently. It would be about this time that the airconditioning was switched on for the year. The airconditioning units favoured by the Institute were dual-purpose. They would provide a much needed flow of cool air in the summer and they were supposed to provide convexion heating during the winter. However, the heating function seemed never to work on any of them and it was rumoured that they were so designed, or more likely fixed, to save on unnecessary heating costs. Obviously, in such a parsimonious institution, a trick was being missed here. It would have been much more economical not to have air-conditioning at all so that any faculty member staying on over the summer for summer school would be forced to buy a cold-air convector of their own or risk heat-stroke. As it was, the provision of air conditioning was regarded by the management as a perk of the job, generously provided out of care for their employees. Nineteenth century English coal mine owners probably felt the same when they provided free water for the children down the pit. Not that the authorities (actually that should be "authority", singular, the Institute being the exclusive possession of its single millionaire owner) needed take any notice of those namby-pamby issues like health and safety at work, concern for which has become the norm in the UK these last few decades. The TRNC government correctly judged that these milksop concessions to fashionable socialistic trends would be inimical to decent profit-making. Just like the salaries of the lecturers and professors, the expense of providing a decent health and safety environment with safe and healthy working conditions was a wasteful cost, a surcharge, as it were, on the business, and therefore best avoided if possible.

About this time, Erkal became our regular taxi driver. He obviously had the good business sense to recognise regular clients when he saw them and he became quite indispensable to us over the remainder of our time on the island. He was a young, friendly personable man of very high intelligence. He would, when we were sitting in the back of his cream Mercedes, explain details of Cypriot culture and politics. In addition to his near-flawless English, he had learnt a few words of French and German from old girlfriends and he would use me for language practice. He did this with a lot of his clients. He knew everyone and he could arrange everything.

"Erkal?"

"Yes, professor?"

"Can you help me, please? I need . . ."

"No problem," he would invariably say, "my brother (or my cousin or my uncle), He is the man you need. I arrange it."

One day Erkal explained to me the economics of the Northern Cyprus taxi trade. The business is seasonal and fares are hard to come by outside the tourist season. So it helps if you have a regular client, like us. The car must be good, so most taxis are late-model Mercedes, usually painted standard taxi-international bland cream. But it is not enough just to buy a car and start working, one must buy a government permit from the Ministry of Transport in Lefkosa. All in all, his total outlay to become a taxi driver had set Erkal back some £65,000 which he was paying back to the bank at a rate of £1300 a month. Given that his car would not set him back more than £40,000, the licence to trade must have accounted for the other £25,000, money extorted either by the government or whoever else was running things.

If this were a government scam, that would be in keeping with other government scams such as the extortionate immigration expenses or the higher levies charged to foreigners to, say, acquire an electricity account or, as Erkal told me, the very high rate charged for speeding fines. This last charge was a clear government rip-off. There were no speed cameras in the towns—indeed, the idea of any sort of traffic management would have been regarded as laughable. There were no pedestrian crossings or traffic lights anywhere. Negotiating the dual carriageways in the centre of Kyrenia as a pedestrian was only for the very quick or the very suicidal. Cars would travel at far higher speeds than the notional national speed limit and pedestrians had to be very fleet of foot indeed if they wished to cross the road and get to the other side alive.

But on one road at least there were speed cameras. On the recently-built modern motorway between Kyrenia and Nicosia a speed camera would report the registration number of any car travelling at more than the legal 65 kilometres an hour, or roughly 40 mph, a speed considerably slower than drivers would drive in built-up areas. But, given that the road was built like an arrow-straight German autobahn specially designed for high-speed driving and given also that that stretch of motorway was also the road to the airport when many drivers would be under time pressure, the cameras were a very nice little money pot indeed, thank you very much. Even the smallest breach of this very low limit would garner an 80 YTL fine. Erkal told us of one taxi driver who had been driven out of business by speeding fines for travelling at what would be regarded as normal motorway speeds in the UK or even as dangerously slow by the drivers on the A8 autobahn between Stuttgart and Würzburg which does not have a speed limit at all.

Because of the various costs of running a taxi business in a low-wage economy, I wondered how Erkal would make it. It is true that he was a clever businessman and he was young enough and strong enough to be able to work more or less 24/7. But this often meant half a dozen airport trips a day, each a round trip of about 120 miles. Add in the costs of his business loan, monthly servicing of the vehicle and saving for its inevitable replacement, plus government taxes and with fuel costing as much as it does in the UK, one wonders how a fair living could be made. But somehow he kept going with charm and good humour, supported by his extended family including his wife, a charming and capable young woman who worked as a hospital midwife, and his two delightful small children who were the apples of his eye.

On occasions when he could not make it, Erkal would send his assistant to drive us. This was Adnam, who had a very personal driving style indeed. Sometimes he would drive too fast, and, if we said anything, which he did not understand anyway, he would brake violently and continue at a snail's pace. If we asked him to speed up, he would hit the accelerator like a Formula 1 driver. Sometimes he would drive on the crown of the road so that we were afraid of oncoming vehicles and at other times he would drive so far over to the left that the left-side wheels would be scraping along the sidewalk. Even though he was a native Kyrenian, he would often get lost or take the wrong turning and he would correct himself by doing a sudden 180 degree hand-brake U-turn and retracing his route on the wrong side of the road. Road junctions and roundabouts were inevitably approached at top speed before an abrupt stamp on the brakes. I feared for our lives and our blood pressure and for Erkal's lovely Mercedes, which purred like a kitten when Erkal was at the wheel and wheezed like a badly-played musical saw under Adnam's guidance. Adnam's entire English vocabulary appeared to consist only of the phrases "one minute", "five minutes", "fifteen minutes", "OK" and "No problem". Even the directions "right", "left", "stop", "straight on" he did not quite understand, so we often found it helpful to resort to our rudimentary Turkish to help him find his way around his native city.

But most disconcerting of all was Adnam's continuous commentary on our trip. He would burble along talking to himself like a character out of an animated cartoon. The tone and the volume would vary according to the driving problems he was struggling with at the moment. If he overshot the turning he might reverse in the main carriageway with a louder vocal accompaniment.

"Er, er, oooAAAAhhh!! ER, er, dribble, dribble . . . AHH!! OH OOH! dribble, dribble . . .", it sounded like to us.

But Adnam was a happy soul and often his self-directed dialogue would be set to music as he added a variable musical intonation to his prattle and we would realise that he was singing to himself. Not quite music as you or I might understand it but obviously melodious to Adnam. We were always relieved when he finally skidded to a halt outside our apartment after a hair-raising, helter-skelter joyride of three miles from the Institute. There he would pull up, jump out of the car and open the door for 'the Professor' as he called me. My wife had to open her own door. Ladies first? What you mean? This is Cyprus!

I wonder what the relationship was between Erkal and Adnam. They were not related or Erkal would have told me. I suspect that Erkal kept him on out of sympathy: it would have been in accord with Erkal's charitable character. Certainly Adnam would find it difficult to find employment unaided. But Erkal, I guess, also found Adnam frustrating and must have lost his temper with him from time to time. On one occasion, Adnam told us

"Me. Finished. Kaput." which was about the longest connected English (Well, two-thirds English.) sentence we ever heard him say. We interpreted it to mean that Erkal had fired him. But a week later he was back was driving us around again, muttering to himself and getting lost in the town he had lived in all his life. It was difficult to help him, not knowing how to say

"No, Adnam, slow down. You"ve missed the turning, you should have taken a left at the last junction." in Turkish.

"OK! No problem! One minute!!" followed by a severe yank on the handbrake.

After every mistake, he would just mutter "Inshallah" to the blaring horns of the other drivers he had mercilessly cut in front of, brake hard and swerve like a stock car driver. Exhilarating but terrifying.

Often I had to phone for a taxi from my office or from home. Ordering a taxi was also a surreal exercise unless Erkal was present to answer the phone. Members of Erkal's family were employed to take orders so my call would often be answered by someone without almost any English at all. The conversation would go something like:

"Effendim!"

"Hello, we want a taxi."

"Taxi? You want taxi?"

"Yes, taxi?"

"You want taxi?"

"Yes please."

"Taxi?"

"Yes, taxi?"

"OK, taxi. Where you now?"

"At our apartment."

"You want taxi your apartment?"

"Yes, our apartment."

"You want taxi, your apartment?"

"Yes."

"You go AIC?"

"Yes."

"You go AIC your apartment?"

"Yes."

"I meet you AIC five minutes."

"No. We want to go to AIC."

"OK. Main gate. Five minutes."

"No, our apartment. Five minutes."

"Apartment? Five minutes!"

"Our apartment. Five minutes."

"OK. No problem."

Naturally, I have had to shorten considerably this account of the taxi-hiring negotiation process. Often it would take five minutes or more of patient diplomacy to finally clinch the deal. What never ceased to amaze us was how often taxi drivers would not know the way around the Kyrenian streets. This obviously did not apply to the mentally alert Erkal, who had been born in Kyrenia and whose talents far exceeded the limited demands of driving a cab in this medium-sized town. But other taxi drivers would need to be told the directions as if they had never heard the address before. Sometimes even the town's landmarks appeared not to be familiar to them

London taxi-drivers only get their licence after they have absorbed what is called 'the knowledge' which is a working mental map of the streets and routes through the capital. Kyrenian taxi-drivers have no such hurdle to overcome before they are allowed out on the streets. Although there are here, of course, other, more stringently financial, barriers to entry to the driving profession. But London has over seven million people and covers hundreds of square miles so there is a lot for the London cabbie to learn.

Not so in Kyrenia, which is about the size of a Dorking or Leamington Spa, so learning the local geography to do one's job should have been easy-peasy. Apparently not, given the number of times that we have had to show not just Adnam, but other taxi drivers as well, the way through the Kyrenian streets.

Eight

There was, by this time, no question of staying in Northern Cyprus for a minute longer than we had to. As one senior international explained to me, "If you stay here for one year, you can hide it on your CV. But any longer than that and your career is permanently damaged."

It was no longer a matter of 'if?' It was now a matter of 'when?' and 'where next?'

Not that I had much to worry about career-wise. I dreamt retirement, I ate, drank and slept retirement. I just wanted a few earning years before I gave up the classroom for ever. What should be our plan? I did what all restless college professors do and that is to start a serious relationship with the job vacancies pages of The Chronicle of Higher Education, the international employment exchange for the academically itinerant. Applying for jobs is much easier in these days of the Internet. One keeps a well-polished CV (or resumé as the Americans call it) together with an easily edited covering letter permanently on file and just send them off by email.

Getting an academic job is largely a percentage game. Ten applications will get you an interested response and ten interested responses should get you a job. So like many forms of cold marketing, it has a hit rate of about 1%. But then it is easy to send out a hundred resumés like spam or junk email. So I applied everywhere—Europe, the Middle East, the USA, for jobs that were right up my street, for jobs that I easily could do given the chance and for jobs that bore only a passing resemblance to what my CV was offering. Getting a job is a bit of a lottery. One could be exactly, perfectly suited to the job on offer and not even be considered because the job advert was merely a legal formality after the home candidate had already been chosen. Other job adverts are just trawling excercises to gather CV's for possible future use. And some job adverts, and those at AIC certainly fell into this category, would be full of blah about 'highly qualified' and 'committed' and 'experienced' when what they really meant was that they would accept any warm human being who could walk upright without his knuckles scraping the ground. In the case of this Institute, the turnover of faculty was such that even the least-capable candidate would soon be gone and whatever problems he had brought with him, or whatever damage and mischief he had created, would soon be gone as well.

I realised that I had reached a point in life when, although I still felt capable of delivering a professional classroom performance, my priorities had changed from the pattern my life had taken up until then which was to stay abreast of my subject and teach it to the best of my abilities. My new need was somehow to cash in on all that knowledge I had collected and built up over a lifetime of scholastic endeavour, and hopefully, in the resonant phrase of the late Reginald Maudling, build up a little pot of money for my old age. I often pondered the question of whether I had made the right life choices all those decades earlier when I was already the primary school star for general knowledge. I suppose it had served me well in one way. It enabled me to escape the slum I was brought up in. Like many of the poor of my generation there had been only two options. The first was that one could learn hard and pass exams and become, if one were lucky, a teacher. Or one could not do too well at school, in which case there was only deadend factory work, petty crime or permanent unemployment.

After a while, the process of fact—and knowledge absorption had become a way of life. With the result that I had spent sixty-odd years building a vast database of knowledge, mostly superficial, on a universality of subjects and, old habits dying hard, I was still reading and absorbing and adding facts to that knowledge edifice, as if still on the run from that early childhood poverty. Education had been my way of getting a better job than those of my classmates at Eustace Street County Primary School who did not pass the exams and thus went on to become factory hands in the local cotton mills or joined the long-term benefit-supported unemployed.

I have frequently heard this argument for education—that it will get you a better job, and that is certainly true. The argument is usually dressed up with phrases like 'education gives you a more fulfilling life', 'education widens ones horizons' etc. All these statements undoubtedly true but they only amount to a restatement of the basic fact that you need education to get a better-paying job. All my life I have waited to hear an intellectual defence of education for its own sake. None, of course exists. A specious argument often made is that higher intellectual interests are, in some way, morally superior to the plebeian tastes of the hoi-polloi and that only those individuals favoured with the appropriate education, either formal or autodidact, would be able to enter this superior, more enlightened and more satisfying world. I find it difficult to understand this argument given that these days access to the arts, literature and music is open to all, of whatever class and educational background. It seems to me that a preference for the Beethoven late string quartets and the National Gallery over punk rock and computer games is nothing more than a straightforward consumer choice which carries absolutely no overtones of superiority whatsoever, neither social, intellectual nor moral.

Having started my career as an idealist who had swallowed all the 'education is a good thing and you can't have too much of it' guff, I had now come full circle to find myself admiring most those academic mercenaries who creamed off the biggest salaries in the most comfortable places. This meant the Middle East and Hong Kong, two places where one gets the best exchange rates between knowledge and cash. So, my resumé-spamming was directed at those colleges which might hold out the best price.

Meanwhile, I had my 66th birthday to celebrate. We decided to try a different restaurant, having been to most of those on offer in central Kyrenia. As part of my preparations I dropped into a roadside barber's for a haircut. In England, I go to unisex hairdressers—I do not feel, like many men, that the barbershop is a haven of machismo where one can escape for a short while, the prying eyes of women, a place where men can talk dirty and gossip about sport. Besides, in my experience, women always cut hair better than men, taking more care and having a better sense of style. But, of course, such enlightened modern attitudes do not hold in Muslim Cyprus so I had to resign myself to whatever is the updated Cypriot equivalent of the short-back-and-sides that I used to get as a child when my mother would press sixpence into my—and my brother's hands and send us off on a Saturday morning once a month to wait in line for the standard crop. This time wife Loydz came with me and she sat at the back of the shop as I was processed by the barber, completely oblivious to the furtive looks she was receiving from the two or three men present. In a unisex hairdresser's in England, she would have been drawn into the discussion about how long, how short, straight or tapered back? But no, it gradually became obvious that the men were extremely uncomfortable at her being there. Women do not go into male hairdressers. Naturally I did not accompany her when she went for her trim and styling. A man sitting in the corner of a women's hair parlour?! Unthinkable!!

We asked Erkal if he could recommend a good restaurant.

"My cousin, he has a wonderful restaurant. The very best on the island! I take you. I will also arrange a car to pick you up at 9 o"clock to bring you home."

He was right. It was a very good restaurant on a leafy terrace overlooking the sea and we ate a fine dinner. As always, the talk turned to when we would be leaving. It was now agreed that we would stay over the summer so that we could travel to Manila for my stepson, Jay's, wedding in late August. Travelling from Cyprus would be less of a journey than if we spent the summer in France and had to travel from Brittany via Paris, and the Middle East. After Erkal's friend had collected us, as promptly as promised, we went for a late drink at the CafeDaD where Albertin kindly presented us with a bottle of wine.

At work, the Institute was gearing up for the annual final exams. Cemaliye, the faculty secretary, brought round a handout with the written instructions for setting them, presenting the papers for printing, the timetable and the invigilation instructions all laid out in well word-processed Turkish. I signed for my copy. Every handout had to be signed for. I often wondered what I was signing away as I was asked to sign for piece of photocopied Turkish. I could have been signing over my soul except that I had already done that long before when I had first taken the Cypriot shilling. No, even a notification that the Human Resources Office would be closed for half an hour next Tuesday would need a handout to which would need to be applied the signature of every faculty member, usually in triplicate. Not that this enthusiastic paper shuffling implied any sort of bureaucratic efficiency. Memos in hard copy were only ever used for trivial, unimportant information and I couldn't understand them anyway. Serious or really useful information was still only transmitted by word of mouth or the student grapevine.

The undergraduate exams themselves followed the same chaotic pattern as the midterms i.e. they were just this side of a total shambles. My graduate classes were no problem and I was able to get a reasonably accurate set of results which did, I thought, accurately reflect the mixed abilities of the graduate students. But my undergraduate course in operating systems was a different matter. As usual, the numbers did not add up but by now the mathematician in me discerned a numerical pattern. The nominal enrollment class size was 30 but the official class list would show between 40 and 50, depending on which version, the paper or electronic, you were reading. The actual numbers attending classes would be about 30 for the first half of the class of which only about 20 would reappear after the first class break at the end of the first hour. These 20 would dwindle away to a hard core of about 15 by the time the class ended. But at the examination, 70 students would arrive to take it, all in possession of the official ID and exam entry certificate. By some weird coincidence, the number showing up for the final exam was exactly the same as the number of seats in the exam room. How they worked this trick, I have no idea. Naturally I did not recognise many of those students for whom this was the first contact with operating systems, but as a friendly student pointed out to me,

"Him, and him, and him. They not students in this class. They borrow ID."

Why anyone should want to borrow an ID to take an exam in a subject about which they knew nothing and in a foreign language was beyond me. They mostly sat at the back and talked or went out for periodic smoke breaks. I did put a mark on their papers when they turned them in but I needn't have bothered. None of them had written anything apart from a few doodles. I gave the best doodle a token 1% for artistic impression.

After the exams had been taken, they were graded. The form was that the results had to be entered into the Registrar's computer. We were also required to submit a paper copy of the results in triplicate. The names on the two lists—the computer's and the paper class list which faculty had created from taking the roster week-by-week—would differ widely. So we were also required to submit another list of the discrepancies, those students who had come to class but were not on the list of those who had paid tuition fees and those students who were on the computer but had never shown up in class. It was then the duty of the registrar and his army of young helpers to reconcile the two lists for every professor and lecturer in good time for the graduation ceremony.

The registrar was particularly hard-pressed at this time. It was quite normal for students to receive diplomas at the graduation ceremony even if, as I recognised from some of my own students, they had actually failed some of their core courses. They would, nonetheless, still receive a degree diploma on the promise that they would subsequently pass the outstanding courses at the graduation makeup exam, where, for a further fee, they would take another shot at the final exam again, the understanding being, nudge, nudge, wink, wink, that they would certainly pass it at the second attempt so that their diplomas would not need to be forfeited. But the real concern of the registrar was to identify those students who had attended classes and had slipped through the payments net. It was quite within the ethos of the AIC that one could get a degree without passing any of the exams which, after all, were merely academic flim-flam. But to get a degree without paying the fees would be downright immoral.

Clearly, we couldn't stay in Ozalay's place much longer. Over a glass at the CafeDaD, Loydz and I decided that the time had come to part company with the famous retired veterinarian and find somewhere else to live. In our routine, Loydz would come into my office after she had finished her housework and she would sit at the back of my class and use the Internet connexion to keep up with her myriad social contacts in The Philippines. No one ever questioned this routine—I suddenly had no boss to report to. TFC was no longer in a position to give me orders and Ergin, my new boss, had a more relaxed view of his management role and left me alone to get on with it. Because Loydz and I were now both going to the Institute at different times, a major problem was the inordinate amount of time and money we were spending on taxi rides. It was a couple of miles to work and cost about ten YTL. Well, it cost ten once we had got to become regular clients of a single driver. Newcomers would be charged up to twenty until they had established themselves—such is the Cypriot way. We felt that it would be a good idea to live a little nearer work. By the end of the spring semester, we wanted to be out of this apartment. So, when we paid the rent at the end of March, we told Ozalay that we would be leaving at the end of June, giving him the three months notice as stated in the contract. Remembering that there is no equivalent phrase in Turkish for 'refundable deposit', we decided that we would do as everyone advised and not to pay the last two months' rent but to forego our two months' deposit instead.

When he had come around for his rent at the end of March, we had told him that we would be vacating the flat at the end of June and that we would not be paying the last two month's rent in return for our deposit. He seemed quite agreeable to this arrangement and also signed the written agreement to that effect which we had prepared for him. But that accord only lasted as long as it took him to get home and explain it to Madame Ozalay. For the rest of the time there we had to endure, almost daily arguments about our irresponsibility, our illegality and our bad faith.

"But, Mr. Payne, you do not understand. The agreement was for a whole year."

"No, Mr. Ozalay, we are allowed, under the contract, to vacate without penalty, as long as we give you fair notice, which we have done."

"No, Mr. Payne. You do not understand. The agreement was for a whole year so you are not allowed to leave until the year is up. You must pay rent until September or I am entitled to keep your deposit."

"Mr. Ozalay, we explained to you that if we give you three months notice, you must return our deposit when we leave. We have given you three months notice and we will be leaving at the end of June."

"Then you must pay up until the end of September or I can keep your deposit."

"We thought you would say that, Mr. Ozalay, so that is why we got you to sign the written agreement that you would take the deposit in place of the last two months rent. You signed it, Mr. Ozalay, and that makes it legally binding on you. So that is what we are going to do."

"No Mr. Payne, that is illegal. You must pay. I have spoken to my wife and she has told me that you must pay. I have already lost one month's rent in commission to the estate agent and I also have tax to pay. If you do not pay up to the end of the year, it is illegal."

"We are not in business with your wife, Mr Ozalay, and your tax is nothing to do with us. If you think you have a case then sue us in the courts."

"Mr. Payne, you are being illegal. I will consult my lawyer and the police."

"Go ahead, Mr. Ozalay, we will see you in court."

This conversation or some variant of it became a standard daily feature of our last two months in Oyzalcin 60. Mr Ozalay would phone or visit or find some excuse to come round and check on something and this piece of dialogue would be reprised on each visit. On one occasion he brought with him the formidable Madame Ozalay who, quite uninvited, wandered around the flat, examining the contents of our cupboards, sniffing disapprovingly and muttering complaints in Turkish to her henpecked husband.

Once we had given notice to the oily Ozalay, all we had to do next was to find somewhere suitable near to AIC. We moved into the new apartment at Pretiji Sitesi (Prestige Site! Ha!!) at the end of June, just as the summer sun was preparing its worst. We packed up all our belongings from Ozalay's flat and put them on the back of the small truck which Erkal had borrowed from his friend. The move was completed in a couple of hours but we still had to endure a final couple of visits from Ozalay himself to check the inventory, to let in the plumbers, to show the place to his daughter, to listen to his complaints that we had not kept him informed about the water leaks and we had not repaired the penetrating damp which had turned our bedroom wall black. I don't know why he expected us to take responsibility for the penetrating damp: it is not the usual duty of a short-term tenant to correct the failings of the jerry-builder who had put up the building in the first place. On each visit we also had to listen to his threats of legal action because we were vacating his apartment before we had been there for a whole year.

We were, it goes without saying, quite relieved to be going. The final ceremony would be the handing over of the keys. Ozalay laid down his terms.

"I will not be back from Istanbul until Sunday, so you must have the keys for me at 8.30 on Sunday evening, with your final utility accounts. And you must go to the shop in the town where you made your agreement to get your TV connection and terminate your contract with them. So I will see you on Sunday evening."

"No, Mr. Ozalay. Sunday evening is not convenient for us. What we will do is leave the keys at the estate agent for you to collect or, if you wish, we can leave them with the gatekeeper of your club at the end of the street. But Sunday evening is impossible."

"But Mr. Payne, this is very bad. You do not understand. You must be there on Sunday evening so that I can take the keys. If you do not do so, it is illegal. You must not give the keys to the estate agent. No, not at all. You must not give the keys to the estate agent."

"If it is illegal, you can always sue us, Mr. Ozalay."

The next morning we dropped off the keys at the office of Select Estates. The young Cypriot woman was sympathetic.

"Oh yes, Mr. Ozalay. A very differen' man. Very differen'. indeed. Big problems. Very bad. Very differen' man. He went to lawyer and lawyer tell him, he not take you court. Mr. Ozalay, we know, always ver', ver' differen'". She meant 'difficult' of course.

After which Pretiji Sitesi promised to be a relief. The small house was within a gated community, about 300 metres from my office. The furniture was a little shabby but we could, we decided, live with it in the short term. How did we come to go there? Well, originally we had been intending to make our escape at the end of June after I had turned in my spring semester grades. But this would have sent me back to France while Loydz went back to her family in Manila to supervise the arrangements for the wedding of Jay, her son. So, given the expense and inconvenience of travelling to western France and then making another trip to Manila for the wedding which was to be held at the end of August, it made more sense to stay on at AIC for summer school, earn a little salary and to travel to Manila from Istanbul.

The landlady turned out to be even more difficult than Ozalay. On our first day in Prestige Site our two next door neighbours soon put us straight about her sterling qualities.

"She's mad," said one.

"Yes, quite mad. Everybody knows about her. One thing you must never do is to give her the money for maintenance. She keeps it for herself. Pay the site management committee directly."

And, yes. They were right. Zehrah the Landlady turned out to be an evil mix of unprincipled greed and mental derangement. We met her only once, when we did the deal to rent from her via Unwin's Estate Agents. She was asking £400 a month, but a spot of haggling by Loydz got her down to a reluctant £375. Then the terms. Would she provide white goods, a new fridge to replace the rusty monster in the kitchen? Of course! What about the washing machine? Yes, a new one will be here when you come! The cooker is not working? We will get it fixed! Everything is very dirty. We will have it cleaned! What about the water and electricity, would they be connected? Yes, of course, no problem! So on that, we shook hands and paid our deposit, which Unwins promised to hold for us and not to turn it over to Zehrah the Landlady.

So, at the end of June, we moved in. Nothing had been done. No white goods, no cleaning, no water, no electricity, no washing machine, no working cooker. Everything was just as it had been. We phoned Zehrah the Landlady.

"What about the washing machine and fridge, you said they would be here."

"They are coming."

"When?"

"Maybe tomorrow, maybe next day."

"What about the water and electricity? They are not connected."

"You must go to the office and make an account."

"But you said there would be no problem. They would be connected."

"You must go to the office and make an account. This is normal."

"But the contract says in Section 6 that it is your obligation to do that."

"This is wrong. I have not read the contract but it is normal that you make an account."

We then steeled ourselves for a trip to the hell's kitchens where the worker elves of the water and electricity utilities were spinning chaos out of chaos.

The office where the electricity accounts are dealt with is a small hall with six counters. One takes a ticket and waits one's turn. This sounds orderly except that the hall is packed to about twice its capacity and no-one takes much notice of the ticket system. But the real business of getting a new account is done upstairs where the single English-speaker holds court in a room measuring about three metres square into which are crowded three desks, thousands of card files and up to a dozen people. When our turn came, we asked about an electricity connection at Prestiji Sitesi. The man sorted through several hundred cards and a couple of ledgers before telling us there was no record of an account at our address. But he would arrange for electricity to be connected. And, much to our surprise, it was. When we arrived back, someone, either the Kumuru Elektrik, the TRNC electricity company, or maybe Tallak, the gardener/oddjob man for Prestige Sites, had replaced the missing fuse with a piece of wire and we had power!

Mains water was a different problem, given as it was to being cut off arbitrarily during summer water shortages. In Cyprus, the absence of mains water is not the sort of seasonal problem to be shared equally by everyone in the community as a communal problem. Oh no, while some houses on the site would have no water, others would have abundant water to spare for car-washing, garden sprinkling and swimming pool filling. The trick is to install a large reservoir tank between the water main and the header tank on the roof and fill it during winter. The header tank and the solar panel heating system would only hold enough water for a couple of days' domestic usage so continual replenishment from the mains was necessary. During the blazing summer, it is essential to take frequent showers and the header tank soon empties. We asked our neighbours how long water shortages usually last.

"Sometimes few hours. Sometimes day. Sometimes five day. You can buy water from tanker."

And so we could. It is an ill wind, or actually an ill heatwave, that does not have a slice of profit somewhere. When the water is cut off, as it had been in Oyzalcin 60 for different reasons, the entrepreneurs go into action. Large tankers which had filled up with municipal water during the winter were suddenly on the streets waiting for the call from parched homeowners. For about ten times the official water price, they would fill up the header tank directly, which they did by sending a small boy up on to the roof with a long hose pipe. There are no health and safety regulations in the TRNC so the Turkish Cypriots still work the hot weather equivalent of sending of little boys up chimneys.

During our stay in Prestiji Sitesi, we often had to call upon Tallak, who seemed, like a good many practical Turkish Cypriots, to be a jack-of-all-trades—electrician, water engineer, landscape gardener, motor mechanic, you name it. Fit and wiry, he was burned a deep chestnut brown by decades of working year-round under the Mediterranean sun. He also sported a permanent friendly smile and he was always eager to help. Rarely have we met anyone so obliging. When he was at a loss to understand what we were saying, he would call on the assistance of his angelic ten-year-old daughter to translate. She was obviously top of her class in English because she was able to translate fluently between English and Turkish, which she did while her father stood by, radiating fully-justified paternal pride.

Over the next few days, the washing machine arrived and the plumbers plumbed it in. It was not new: it was second hand and broken. We tried using it but after we had paid through the nose to fill up the header tank and made the mistake of going out, we had come back to discover that the machine had run through its washing cycle several times until our new fill of water had been completely depleted. Similarly the electric cooker was also broken and we were down to one small gas ring for hot food and drinks. The electricians who came to fix it were astonished that that cooker model was still in use, so old was it.

After a week of this, Loydz left for her trip to Manila, where she could see her family and attend to the million and one things which needed to be done to ensure that the wedding of her son would be a success. Which, of course it was. But in the meantime, I was left to live in the house with limited cooking and washing facilities, no air conditioning and with only intermittent water and electricity. I was able to escape to the Institute each day where it was cool and I could eat. Laundry had to be done by hand and I used the stove only for making coffee. As in many hot countries, one does not drink the mains water so I had water for drinking delivered in large 15-litre plastic containers for transfer to litre bottles which I then cooled in the fridge. One drinks lots of water when the midday temperature is over 40C. Even the 300 metre walk to my office would leave me breathless, wringing with sweat and dehydrated. My daily water consumption would easily top five litres.

We had given notice that we would be leaving when we paid our first month's rent at the end of June and I had been hoping that we would see out the tenancy without any further problems with the dreaded utilities companies. We almost made it too but just before I was due to go to Manila and join my wife, we were hit by a double whammy, the first a water bill for 900 YTL, including the 850 YTL run up by the previous tenant.

And it was also just about this time that I had a couple of Sunday morning visitors. Two smart young women, one very much in charge.

"Hello, we are from Office of Revenue and Taxes."

"Yes?"

"You rent this house?"

"Yes."

"Who from?"

I showed her my rental agreement.

"Your landlady, where is she?"

"I don't know. We spent a lot of time calling her but she no longer returns our calls."

"Why you call her?"

"You want the full list? Washing machine, water supply, electricity . . . Here's her phone number."

"Where she live? You know?"

"Round here somewhere, but I don't know exactly where. Why not ask my neighbours? They will know."

"We will."

I later found out that my neighbours were only too happy to grass up Lunatic Zehrah to the tax gatherers.

Our problems with this apartment also showed us that even long-term expatriates will eventually turn native and join in the refundable/ non-refundable scam. After the struggle against the oleaginous Ozalay, we had chosen to rent our second apartment from a British estate agency. Indeed, Unwins Estate Agents had once traded property throughout the

British Empire, although lately it was much reduced from its glory days when they would house district commissioners and their memsahibs. Northern Cyprus had now become one of its last redoubts. But all the staff were British and we, perhaps naively, were expecting the business ethics of the Tunbridge Wells High Street. So we read the contract carefully and asked for written confirmation that our deposit would be held by them, Unwins, and not made a gift of it to the landlady. No problem—we will hold it, we were assured by the manager, a retired Royal Military Policeman,—safe as the Bank of England. That is until the same two young women who had visited me also paid Unwins a call to find out why our landlady had not been paying tax on her rental income. By this time three months rent had been paid and three months tax had not been deducted by Unwins, as they were obliged to do. So Unwins had to pay the back tax on behalf of the landlady. Because of their neglect, poor Unwins were now £112.50 out of pocket and since the only money left in the kitty was our deposit, what could be more natural, or more Cypriot, than that they should help themselves to £112.50 of ours. Only fair, isn't it? So when we turned over the keys to Unwins to retrieve our deposit, we were short-changed by that amount. That was the end of our dealings with both Unwins and Zehrah the Mental-Hospital-Mad Landlady. We were angry at the way we had been treated by both of them and we thought that was probably the end of it. Except that Mad Zehrah made one long last intemperate threatening phone call to me while I was socialising with some of my colleagues.

"You must immediately come to see me and bring with you all your utilities bills and your receipts for the maintenance. You must today pay me your rent and I must inspect the apartment and its inventory. You must . . . You must . . . You must . . .".

She continued issuing commands like this for several minutes until I switched the phone off.

We did not get our £112.50 back of course, but it gave us just a little satisfaction that Unwins would be paid back for their duplicity by a series of unpleasant daily visits and phone calls from the angry madwoman of Prestige Sites.

Manila was nice and comparatively cool after the trials of the summer and the wedding of my stepson Jay, to Angel was a great success. I was able to meet Loydz' new grandson, Thyriz, for the first time and Loydz and I were able to spend a wonderful week just relaxing together before the long trip back to Cyprus with all the problems of packing up and finding a new apartment.

Surprisingly to us, this next move went well and after three days in a cheap but decent-enough hotel, we were able to move our possessions on the back of Erkal's friend's truck, to a newish, clean well-appointed apartment on the other side of town near the Institute's halls of residence with their shuttle bus to the campus.

This apartment came with utilities accounts in order, a full working kitchen including washing machine and Lydia, a jolly, always-smiling, property manager, who actually did her job. The absentee landlord actually volunteered to lower the rent by £25 because the swimming pool maintenance was on hold and the pool had been emptied. I reckoned that we would not be using the swimming pool anyway given that our neighbours included several of my lady students in front of whom I did not wish to disport myself.

Nine

When we got back to Kyrenia from Manila, we were able to catch up on the news from the Institute. During the summer there had been great changes. The old Rector and the Dean of Business and Economics had both been fired along with twenty or thirty faculty members. The new Rector, a senior Turkish academic with an international reputation in health management was spearheading a drive to give AIC a presentable academic profile ahead of the upcoming accreditation applications. Even the general secretary, a close friend of the owner's, was, it was rumoured, going to be demoted to a lectureship in economics. Next to the owner, the general secretary was the most feared and unpopular man in the place. It was alleged that he had got his degrees at a very fair price indeed, but that is probably just hearsay. Not that getting letters after one's name by short-circuiting the long tedious route of academic achievement is an entirely Cypriot activity, of course. There is a well-known story which does the rounds of British academia concerning an establishment in the industrial north of England which had progressed over a couple of decades from second-rate technical college to third-rate polytechnic to fourth-rate university. Immediately after the final metamorphosis, the senior administrators had all awarded themselves honorary senior doctorates which they then proceeded to use as official and personal titles.

In the summer cull, TFC had been offered a teaching position in the faculty of education, presumably the one department on which she had not yet worked her malicious magic. When she had turned it down, she, too, was fired, and the new Rector made me Head of Management Information Systems. But before the start of the fall semester and my new responsibilities, Loydz and I had work to do.

By now it was a year since we had seen our house in Brittany. All year I had been having nightmares about what would be happening to it. I imagined break-ins by local *cambrioleurs,* or invasions by the large population of small animals who live under the terrace or maybe a flooding or fire, squatters or a dozen other possibilities. So after we had recovered from the long flight back from Manila, we thought it about time either to visit the house to put our fears to rest or to continue to compound our worries.

Northern Cyprus is a prison. The main exit is via Turkey, although European citizens with EU burgundy passports are allowed to travel to the Greek side as part of the European Union. But for Turkish Cypriots, those born in Turkey and all those people who come from that part of the world which is not the EU or the USA or a few countries like Syria or Pakistan, travelling into and out of the Turkish Republic of Northern Cyprus is about as difficult as getting in and out of East Berlin was during the Cold War.

But we had to go to France for at least three days and we had little time to do it so we first checked the times and availability of flights out of North Cyprus via Istanbul. We could travel directly to London Stansted, with just a stay-on-the-plane touchdown in Turkey, and then get a local flight from Stansted to France but the timing meant we would have overnight stays in London in both directions. Or we could change to a direct Paris flight at Istanbul.

We don't like changing planes in Istanbul. The Turkish authorities, alone among the world's airports in my experience, operate a greedy little racket for people who are changing planes. They call it 'the transit visa'. Every passenger moving from one airline to another has to pay a tax to do so. The tax is variable according to the nationality of the traveller and the first thing an incoming passenger sees is a big board listing the tariffs. Beneath the board is an office where grim-faced immigration officials collect their loot. There is no logic to the pricing system—European citizens pay different charges depending on where their passports were issued e.g. Frenchmen pay €20 but Dutchmen only €15. Canadians are particularly hard hit with a tariff of 65 Canadian dollars. What is it about Canada that the Turks don't like, I wonder? Naturally, as in most parts of the third world, hard currency is preferred to the local stuff, so the tariffs are listed in pounds sterling, US dollars or euros. The last time I passed through Istanbul en route for Manila, and I sincerely hope it will be the last time I am ever in Istanbul airport, I asked the hatchet-faced tax-vulture behind the desk if I could pay in Turkish Lira. She agreed only reluctantly and charged me 20% above the sterling exchange rate and that only after she had made an elaborate fuss about not having the right change.

An additional reason for not wanting to stopover in Istanbul is the problems that Loydz always has with immigration. Every time we come up against immigration control, there is great consternation when, as a citizen of The Philippines, she must always be carefully checked for her eligibility to enter or leave the country whether she has the correct papers or not. My reading of world history and geopolitics is that her country is one of the most peaceable enemy-free countries in the world. It is like a sort of southeast Asian version of Iceland or The Netherlands, on good terms with almost the whole of humanity, to whom it supplies a generous workforce of friendly hard-working seamen, domestic workers, nurses and child carers. But when it comes to immigration officials, my Filipina wife is treated like a fourth rate human being despite her being a super-respectable middle-aged housewife married to an English professor. Like most Filipinas, she is absolutely no threat to the state apparatus of any country and, since she is financially reliant on me, she will never need to impose on the hospitality of any host country. In these paranoid times when we are all supposed to be engaged in the war against terror, I can assure the international brotherhood of immigration policemen that no, she is not intending to set up any terrorist cells and there really is no room in her underwear for guns or explosives.

Everyone despises bureaucrats but immigration bureaucrats are surely the most contemptible of them all. For the most part they are low-ranking policemen with enormously disproportionate power over people's lives which they can destroy arbitrarily with the stroke of a pen. No visa? Then go home! Exit permit a day late because the plane couldn't take off? Then go to your embassy five hundred miles away and pay a hundred dollars to get a stamp in your passport. If you should be possessed of a vindictive, obstructive, misanthropic personality combined with a dog-like obedience to inhuman, perverse and arbitrary rules, then immigration official is definitely the career for you.

The immigration jobsworths also have the power to ease the path of the traveller should they wish to but they will rarely do so unless they are forced into a corner and left with no option. For example, I regularly travel to The Philippines without a visa and the immigration officials there will give me an open-ended visa for a whole year not because they have the power to do so but exceptionally, unlike their malevolent brothers in other countries, the Philippine immigration service does not see itself as the xenophobic face of government. They even smile!!

So after several bad experiences, travel via Istanbul had become our itinerary of last resort. So how to get out of the gulag that is North Cyprus? A quick google found us a flight which fitted our schedule and, unlike travel via Istanbul, was reasonably priced. The only problem was that it was going from Larnaca in the Greek south of Cyprus, from where I, as an EU citizen, could travel, but my wife, as a Filipina, could not. Now the Greek Cypriot immigration apparatus is quite as bone-headed and inhumane as its Turkish counterpart and Loydz had already made several applications for a visa to visit the Greek side of Cyprus at the Embassy of the Republic of Cyprus in Manila. They had always taken her $50 and they had always refused her. Most likely because, although it is their 'policy' not to give reasons, of the Turkish stamps in her Philippine passport.

But we had already tested Greek immigration obduracy a couple of times by taking trips through the United Nations 'Green Line' from Turkish Lefkosa to Greek Nicosia. The first time we were stopped and questioned before getting in but the second time we were just waved through. Reasoning that this inconsistency could well work for us, we bought tickets from Larnaca to Paris, rented a car at Hertz in Paris and booked a driver to take us south to the airport. We had heard of a thaw in Turkish-Greek relations with high-level talks 'well-advanced' and of the opening of Ledra Street connecting Turkish and Greek Nicosia as well as the good news of Greek Cyprus's signing up to the European Union's Schengen Treaty. With so much promise of a new liberal attitude, why, we wondered naively, would the immigration police make it difficult for us, apolitical nationals of friendly countries, with no interest apart from academic in the politics of Cypriot partition?

How wrong we were. Our driver arrived at 5.30am and we drove the 75km or so to Larnaca stopping only to show our passports at the Greek entrance gate in Nicosia. For some reason, I never understood what, our driver was a rare Turk with the freedom to move between both communites. At the crossing point, the police detained us for ten minutes or so to deliberate over the exotic strangeness of the Philippine passport with its multitude of Turkish and European stamps. But after a quick phone call from the junior to his sergeant we were let through with the admonition that we would be well advised, on coming back, to bring with us, our marriage contract and evidence of European domicile such as the title deed of our French house.

Our troubles really began when we got to the emigration desk at Larnaca airport.

"Oh, dear, this is very bad. You have no visa for our country. You should not be here."

The speaker was a very new immigration official, who looked about twelve years old and who was still, he told us, an undergraduate student. What joy for him, on a hot humid morning, to escape the tedium of waving through an endless stream of English holidaymakers! Suddenly he could exercise more power than he had ever dreamed of. A helpless Filipina woman was at his bureaucratic mercy! Wouldn't that be something to tell his mates in the student bar!

"But your colleague in Nicosia let us through"

"He shouldn't have," said the youngster, "this is very bad."

By this time, several other policemen had joined in and soon there was a cacophony of excited arguments in Greek. The gist seemed to be that the older sergeant wanted us to be granted an exit but the younger men were holding out for us to produce whatever document they thought we should have. The boy wonder explained it to us.

"You know the history of our country?"

"Of course."

"You know the history of our country? The northern part is an illegal state and you cannot go there and come here."

He then proceeded to a recitation of the history of Cyprus since independence, partition and the illegal Turkish invasion. It sounded like an elective class from his undergraduate degree course in obstructive self-importance. I cut him short.

"It is not our fight. We are just passing through."

"Ah," he riposted in triumph," but you do not have the right papers!"

"What would you like us to do? After all, you let us into your country."

"That was a mistake."

There was then another ten or fifteen minutes of flicking though Loydz" passport, of excited telephone calls and conferences with other policemen. Finally, he decided that we had been humiliated enough, that our obligatory obeisance had been prolonged sufficiently. Now he was ready to move on to the next stage, magnanimity.

"OK, I will stamp your wife's passport so you can go to Paris,." and here his voice turned stern as he wagged his finger

"But immediately you get there, you must go to our embassy there and get a visa."

"Also, if you want to come to our country again, you must always have the proper papers! You must also make sure that you have proof of where you live and your marriage contract. Do you understand?"

I was about to reply "Yes sir, of course sir, whatever you say sir," but as a professor and old-age pensioner, I never think it dignified to inflict my sarcasm even on the most supercilious of my freshmen students which, had he been born a few miles further north on the Turkish side of the Green Line, he might well have been. So we went through the X-ray scanner and submitted ourselves to that partial undressing in public and to the gropings of the security police, which now seem to be mandatory in these paranoid times, even for those not travelling cattle class.

Brittany in September turned out to be as beautiful as ever. The weather was nicely cool, which was a great relief after Cyprus. The soft rain and the gentle autumnal sunshine were a delight after four months under a cloudless sky and a vertical sun. The house was still in good shape. It had not been invaded by rodents, the soot in the chimney had not descended to the sitting room, there was no damp—only a few cobwebs, and no broken window panes. We disturbed a mouse in the nest it had built on the steps down to the garage and I felt like a West Bank bulldozer driver as I destroyed its home. But four or five hours of sweeping and cleaning soon reversed a year's neglect.

We transferred money at the bank to pay our French bills, we redirected our mail for another year, we renewed the contract for storage of our furniture and we spoke to our estate agents, one of whom provided us with copies of our title deeds which, the Greek Cypriot police had assured us, would suffice, with our marriage contract, to get us back into Greek Cyprus. The house had, by this time, been on the market for a year without stimulating any interest so the estate agent, as estate agents are wont to do, suggested lowering the price. The market for properties was, she told us, 'slow'. Estate agents follow a universal script, in whatever language they are working. I tried some Occam's Razor logic here. If no-one is buying houses at all, I asked, possibly naively, then what does it matter what price we put on it? She assured me it would make all the difference and it would sell at the right price. I have now come to the conclusion that, far from being deserving of the opprobrium they usually come in for, estate agents are indeed worthy of our deepest respect and admiration for their unfailing blind optimism in the crudest workings of marketplace whatever the actual financial and economic facts about the real dire state of the housing market might be.

We also did some shopping for items which are unobtainable or overpriced in Kyrenia such as bathroom toiletries and we enjoyed a couple of splendid French dinners—the last taste of good cuisine for at least a year, we feared.

Then, after driving back to Paris and dropping off the car at Charles de Gaulle airport, we boarded the plane for Milan and Larnaca. The first likely point of trouble would be at Milan since these days airline check-in staff have a dual role as frontier guards. We were primed for trouble after encountering a young Algerian boy with a Schengen visa who was going to Larnaca to get married. All evidence of the purpose of his visit was in his luggage which had been booked through from Algiers to Cyprus. He was in tears as he tried to explain to the unfeeling check-in girl that his fiancée was waiting for him, the arrangements had all been made and he could not even call her. Ever helpful, the check-in girl gave him the address and phone number of the Greek Cyprus Embassy in Italy where he could get a visa. It was now Sunday afternoon and the Embassy is in Rome, halfway down the leg of Italy. But what the hell, we're an airline: it's not as though we are in the people business!

When our turn came, the same girl asked us if we live in Larnaca.

"No, Kyrenia." and she let us through.

We did not, of course, give her the Turkish name, Girne, of our home city in Northern Cyprus and she clearly thought that Kyrenia, which was once a Greek city but is now wholly Turkish, is in the European south of Cyprus, not the alien north. So much for Italian geography teaching.

So just one more enormous hurdle, the entry at Larnaca airport. It took an hour. The immigration cops on duty were the very same ones who had caused us so much grief on our way out. Like predatory animals, they were waiting to pounce. And, sure enough, they took us out of the line and into the back office and after a few minutes argy-bargy while they asked us exactly the same questions which we had been asked on the outward trip, they then ordered us to sit in the air side of the arrivals hall while they decided what to do about us and our implicit threat to the security of the Greek Cypriot state. The immigration cops came and went with our papers while we sat watching planeload after planeload (I counted six.) of British holidaymakers breezing through with just a casual wave of the magical maroon pasteboard. A whole planeload would pass by in less than two minutes. No passenger was stopped—each passport was examined in a microsecond

It is easy to recognise them as the British at play—badly dressed, ill-shapen and sunburned scarlet. Here and there could be observed the modern British couple—she a bottle blonde in high heels, half-dressed as if for the night club and accompanied by her shaved bald consort, fat stomach contained in a singlet and clutching a beer can. The whole ensemble was set off by his'n'her matching tatoos and a pair of obese unruly infants who would periodically incite their mother's chastisement.

"Chardonnay! Jermaine! If I've bloody told you once!"

All these passed by while we waited for the verdict of the phalanx of Greek Cypriot frontier guards. They came out several times to ask if we had proof of domicile.

"Yes, here are the title deeds of our house in France. We are European residents like you."

"We don' understand this."

"It's in French. That's where we live."

"This is ver' bad."

Then they needed to see our marriage contract. Again, puzzlement over a Philippine marriage contract.

"What is this?"

"Our marriage contract."

We pointed at the sergeant who had kept us waiting four days before when we were departing.

"Him! That man there! He told us that if we bring proof of domicile, and our marriage contract, there would be no problem."

"But you do not have the right documents. This is ver' bad."

"Cyprus Airways brought us here."

"They shouldn't have. They will have three thousand euro fine for doing this."

Where am I, I thought? Possibly I'm in some weird parallel universe where the laws and rules have a sort of protean fluidity, applied arbitrarily at the whim of whichever bureaucrat you are dealing with. It is a feeling I had many times in Cyprus. We have discovered though, and this was what we had been banking on, that if you play dumb and do not make the mistake of losing your temper by telling them just how much you despise bloody-minded, obstructive and dim-witted bureaucrats, then the problem mysteriously transfers itself from you to them. At first, they had the upper hand and if they really wanted to keep us out of their country they should have made a decision immediately. But they did not act swiftly enough and so during the hour when we were kept prisoner, the problem gradually and subtly stopped being our problem and became theirs. The immigration cops now had a dilemma. What to do? To keep this respectable middle aged couple prisoners in the immigration hall? Where would they sleep? To find a hotel for them and guard it until the wife could be put on a plane for deportation to Manila? Since none of immi-cops had the rank for such a radical, if logical, solution, and it being Sunday night, when their bosses would be at home and undisturbable, then the easiest way to get rid of the problem would be simply to pick up the rubber stamp and bang it down on a free page in Loydz' passport. Job done, at a stroke.

Obviously, we might have been able to speed up the process if we had taken one of the men aside and slipped a little 'gift' into his hand. But bribery is trickier than it looks when you see it done in the films. Sizing up the most likely bribee, isolating him from his colleagues and getting the price right are difficult arts to master and, I reckoned, I would probably get it wrong. No, I think we called it right. Sit things out and they would eventually get tired of us.

There is another factor. Deep down, below the blind obedience of the petty official and his need to be seen to be taking his job seriously by choosing the occasional arbitrary victim for his spite, there is a recognition that detaining the sort of people who will demand to see their ambassadors and the local foreign ministry and who will have the confidence, as well as no compunction, happily to turn a small event into a major international incident is, in the long run, more trouble than his job is worth.

Easier to let them go with a little stern face-saving admonition really, isn't it? Which is what they did. We had to endure the five minutes of finger-wagging and ostentatious magnanimity but that is standard and then we were through! Fortunately our driver had waited for us, our luggage was still on the carousel and all, we concluded, would now be plain sailing.

Not much more eventful happened that evening. Except, that is, the drive back to Kyrenia took rather longer than we had planned on account of the driver's having brought a navigator to help him find his way through Nicosia. This navigator knew Nicosia like the back of his hand, so we were able to see most of it that evening as we spent a happy hour driving round and round its suburbs in search of the Green Line frontier post. The navigator's mental map of Nicosia, we soon found out, was actually dated 1975.

When we got back to our apartment, we discovered that several of the other apartments in the block had become occupied in the few days that we had been away and the students next door were in the throes of a party. It was then that we discovered someone had stolen the main fuse to our electricity supply. No coffee, no hot shower, no air-conditioning. Sweet dreams, the end of a perfect Cypriot day.

The next day was to be my first day in the new job as Head of MIS. But before I could go to work there was the problem of the electricity. We called Erkal, our ever-resourceful taxi-driver, who had the very friend who could solve our problem. The electrician arrived shortly after nine and we explained to him that someone had stolen our main fuse.

"Yes, that's what they do here. This is Cyprus."

He said this almost proudly as if fuse-stealing were some kind of national achievement for which Cyprus is world famous. Like a Brazilian bragging about football or the samba.

His solution was Cypriot-pragmatic. He simply moved the fuse for the stairwell to our meter and put a piece of wire in place of the stairwell fuse. Five minutes and 20 YTL later he was gone and we had electricity. Safety regulations? What safety regulations? This delay meant that I started my first day in my new job by turning up late. Fortunately everyone else was also late so it was not noticed. Most of my colleagues in the cramped offices of the Faculty of Business and Economics were still absent and the whole Institute still had its funereal air of summer indolence.

Cypriots are not known for their business flair or entrepreneurial enterprise so their business dealings tend to a way of making a quick buck by application of simple peasant cunning. This is why they have mastered the art of the non-returnable returnable deposit as tried on us by Mr.

Ozalay. The electricity company, Kumuru Elektrik, operates a particularly clever version of the scam. Before you can be hooked up for electricity, you need an electricity account. It is, of course, not possible to take over an existing account because the previous tenant of your apartment will not have paid his bill and you would then be responsible for it. No, if you are lucky enough to get one of the rare places where the electricity has been paid up, then you will need to visit the crowded squalid hell-hole that is the head office of the Kyrenia electricity supplier. Here is where you pay your deposit in cash and no cheques, if you don't mind. In 2007 the charge for a new account was a straight 175 YTL for everyone, Cypriot and non-Cypriot alike. But sometime during the following year, it was decided that, because so many people were not paying their bills at the end of a tenancy, the deposit would need to be raised to 250 YTL for local people and 850 YTL (approximately £380) for those dastardly foreigners. But surely, I hear you ask, the money will be safe, given that Kumuru Elektrik is a public utility? Indeed it is safe and they will return it after you have settled your final bill, vacated your residence and left the country. It will be returned to you in the form of a cheque, drawn on a local bank and only cashable there, which you can collect from the hell-hole about a month after your departure to Chicago or Manchester or wherever!! Isn't that clever?

Again, the local people have a solution. First, expatriates, if they are bothering to operate legally, need to get a local Cypriot to pay the lower deposit for them, which many will do for a small consideration. When an account is closed and the current is cut off, the company removes the fuse from the fuse box. So what a lot of the locals do is to connect up the electricity by stealing a fuse from an adjacent fusebox or just short circuiting the electricity meter using a length of wire. As we saw, your friendly local electrician will help you do this for only 20 YTL. All of which explains the Cypriot pre-eminence in the ancient and noble art of fuse-stealing—a skill learnt at one's father's knee.

Meanwhile back at AIC, I was still trying to get access to my new office. TFC had taken the office keys home with her when she had been fired and there were no spares. The faculty rooms had a double locking system. There is a regular lock with Yale keys and there is an electronic lock activated by a sensor to read the faculty ID card. So, I went to the IT Department and the redoubtable IT Manager, king of all things computerised within the Institute.

"This ID opens Room TP103 and, now that I am Head of Department I need to get this ID changed so that I can get into the office next door, so can you change the code on it please?"

"No." he said with a smile.

"Why not?"

"Mehmet is not here." he said with an even wider smile.

"When will he be back?"

"Not till after bayram."

Bayram is the local term for a holiday, in this case the upcoming week's holiday to mark the end of Ramadan.

By this time he was grinning from ear to ear.

"And!"

Here he paused theatrically, and said, with an expression of pure delight,

"Then we are going to change the system!!!"

"So how am I going to get in and out of my office?"

"Well," he riposted, "you are just going to have to ask the cleaners to let you in!!"

I had made his day.

Later in the week, by some mysterious process, the key arrived courtesy of the faculty secretary, Cemaliye, an infinitely resourceful woman, who hinted that someone may have telephoned TFC to ask her to return the Institute's property. By Friday I was in occupation and Loydz very kindly accompanied me to the Institute to use her considerable skills for organisation, and her natural tidiness, to turn a scruffy office into something resembling a decent study.

I also managed to get my shoes repaired courtesy of Erkal. For a year I had looked in vain for a shoe repairer. I could see that the local population was used to wearing shoes and that there were also plenty of shoe shops around. Stands to reason that there must be a cobbler somewhere who repairs shoes. Asking at the shoe shops drew a blank response.

"Shoe repairs? No, we don't know . . ."

Clearly inquiring about shoe repairers in a shoe shop is the sort of stupid question only a stupid foreigner would think of stupidly asking. I had met the same response a year earlier when I had visited the same shops to ask if they sold shoe laces. On that occasion, I had only found some at about the seventh shoe shop I had visited. And at about £3 a pair, I thought they were a tad on the expensive side. But shoe repairs? No chance, or so it seemed, until I remembered to ask the capable Erkal, who knew of two shoe repairers, one east of the town and the other down the coast at the nearby village of Lapta.

'There are only two cobblers in Northern Cyprus. One is my cousin. The other is my uncle. I take them."

I handed over five or six pairs of down-at-heel shoes and lo and behold! A day later, for the princely sum of 45 YTL, about twenty pounds, all my shoes had been carefully re-heeled. The quality was good—they were still neat and tidy a year later.

The struggle against the malign forces at work on this island is relentless. But this week, to use a football analogy, we had achieved a hard-fought draw. I had a decent office and I had finally discovered a way to get my shoes repaired. Who could ask for anything more?

Ten

Registration began in the first week of October, but I did not expect too many students to show up, it being the end of Ramadan which is celebrated by three-day family parties—the "bayram". The Institute was officially open for half a day on the Monday and Reban agreed to go in and register any students who came in before it closed at lunchtime so that faculty and staff could go home early. I did not go in because we were planning a trip to Karpaz—the sparsely inhabited area at the tip of the Cyprus panhandle and I could see no point in going into an empty Institute to await the non-appearance of students who would be getting themselves into party mood and would not show up for another week anyway.

The outgoing Institute general secretary did not share my view, though, and did a head count of all faculty present on the Monday morning, possibly in retaliation for his approaching loss of status with his impending demotion to mere lecturer. I find the thought of someone checking up on my attendance quite demeaning and had I known he was going to do it, I would have put a notice on my office door to make it clear that I was not in and what was he going to do about it? I haven't punched a clock card since I was seventeen years old, some fifty years before, and I will not report to some talentless bureaucrat who needs to find things to make other people do in order to justify his misanthropic existence.

The rise of the administrator in academia has been exactly in parallel with the decline in status of the professoriat. Management and even academic decisions in most institutions of higher education are now made, not by the professors, but by a cadre of administrators who are, often as not, failed academics themselves. Even decisions on purely scholastic matters, such as, for example, which lecturer would be best qualified to teach a particular course, or whether a particular student had plagiarised their PhD thesis, will often be taken by members of this group without reference to the professor of the subject under whose area of expertise the matter might properly fall.

There is a peculiar tortuous logic in this. It is widely believed that someone who cannot cut it as a lecturer in a real academic discipline must, the reasoning goes, have some compensating skills as an administrator. There is a particular type of the species I have met many times in my career as a university teacher. With a poor first degree and, possibly, a master's degree achieved with great difficulty, this type embarks on a career as a university lecturer. Soon, though, the struggle to keep up to date with their subject and their natural lack of intellectual curiosity means that they soon find themselves falling behind their contemporaries. The promised papers do not get written and the PhD takes longer and longer to complete, often being dragged out for a decade or more or just abandoned altogether. It is from the ranks of these mediocrities that the administrative layers of universities are usually drawn. By being seen to be busy with intellectually light-weight make-work such as reports, memos and committees, even the most obtuse scholastic dullard can find his or her place in the sun. Or, as H.L. Mencken famously put it ," And those who can't teach, administrate."

In some universities, the time-servers and the totally talentless can ascend to the sort of level where they can award themselves honorary degrees, an honour which was formerly reserved for the truly distinguished—scholars, statesmen, diplomats and so on, but which are now given routinely to film actors, guitar players and footballers. Along with these gaudy luminaries of popular culture, a leavening of unworthy academic bureaucrats, whose only discernible quality is personal ambition, can also pick up some doctorate or other such as "Doctor of the Universiy of West Bromwich in honoris causa".

I did not show up for rollcall. Instead Loydz and I tried unsuccessfully to rent a car for the holiday period. When the car rental company did not bother to return our calls or to acknowledge our order and when the clouds brought a heavy downpour and especially when we saw the amount of traffic going home for the bayram, we abandoned all thoughts of Karpaz, partook ourselves of a pleasant lunch and then went home. We decided instead to take a free trip on the Institute bus organised by the jovial and expansive International Director, Vice-Chancellor Rick, on behalf of new, or my case, newish, faculty members.

It was a very enjoyable day out. Rick proved to be an expert on the history and geograhpy of Cyprus and with his booming extrovert personality he was an excellent tour guide and host. The tour took in the ancient Greco-Roman ruins of Salamis, the tomb of Saint Barnabas, the patron saint of Cyprus, and a trip around downtown Famagusta where our indefatigable leader bought all ten of us icecream. A wonderful day!

Friday was back at work after the bayram. I went into the office to clear off some of the paperwork concerned with grade changes, late exam results and summer school reports. I also had to do paperwork for new faculty and try to rearrange a visit from senior members of an exchange college in England. I had been kept away from the running of the department during the disastrous chaotic reign of TFC so I found myself with much to learn and catch up on. The paperwork was not difficult. Indeed, most of it was just common sense but in a bueaucracy it tends to increase relentlessly. One of the reasons for this is the way bureaucracies increase their management numbers quadratically. Not exponentially—that would be too cynical a word. No, quadratically-the reason being that communication is the main function of administration and management and the number of communication links increases as the square of the number of communicators.

I also registered a couple of students, although I was proved correct in my estimation that most students would extend their holiday over the weekend. But I did have just the one student registration to test my patience. There was a knock on my door. I opened it and a student strode past me.

"Come in."

No reply.

"Are you here to register?"

Again, no reply.

"What do you want?"

Still no reply.

"Register?"

A grunt this time, which I assumed meant yes.

"What is your name?"

He pointed to the computer and grunted again.

I pulled up the list of student names and scrolled down until he pointed to his. He spoke.

"Lesson!"

I saw that he was listed as eligible to take a standard clutch of second year courses in computer programming, web page design, mathematics and economics—the regular sophomore load in the MIS Department.

"Shouldn't you do English first?"

A blank look.

"English?"

"Ah Inglis! No Inglis. Inglis gone! Lesson."

"Have you completed Foundation English?"

"Inglis! Finish!"

I brought up his transcript on the computer. It showed that he had indeed taken two semesters i.e. a whole academic year of Foundation English but there were no grades posted. I showed him.

"Look! Grade, No! GPA, No!"

He muttered something in Turkish. I think it meant that he would bring his Foundation English Diploma on Monday, after the weekend.

"Monday?"

A grunt.

"Monday?"

Another grunt. I used one of my few words of Turkish.

"Pazartesi?"

His face lit up.

"Pazartesi! OK! Pazartesi!"

Something to look forward to on Monday and to prepare for over the weekend.

And sure enough, there he was on Monday, with his diploma showing that he was now able to follow classes in English which had been awarded to him by the Department of Foundation English.

"Lesson!"

"What. Do. You. Want. To. Study?"

"Lesson!"

I pointed to the list of classes. He picked out one of the hardest courses, software engineering.

"This! I study!"

By this time I was past caring, so I signed him up for software engineering, whether he could pronounce the title of the course or not.

The tourist trade to Northern Cyprus has its own seasons. Older couples stroll the Kyrenia promenade in the cool months of spring and autumn, having travelled on off-season deals. During the summer when the schools are closed, families occupy the beaches and the hotel swimming pools. Almost all of the visitors are British: one rarely hears any other foreign language than English. No German, or Russian as you might hear in other parts of the Mediterranean.

But the year had not been a good year for tourism, or the local hoteliers. Many hotels struggled to fill their rooms and there were mass protests by hotel-keepers at the Ministry of Tourism. Many hotels were forced to close permanently. The reasons were not difficult to find. Apart from the general economic slowdown which had forced many British families to forego their usual summer holiday in the sun, travel costs between Standsted and Ercan, the major airport in the TRNC, had been raised substantially for both scheduled and charter flights. As a result, Northern Cyprus had lost a good part of its tourist trade to Spain and Italy.

Direct flights to and from London Stansted had only recently been instituted. Until a few years ago, passengers had to stop off in Istanbul and endure the additional costs of the Istanbul immigration transit visa racket. But lately, some enterprising carriers had managed to get around this by providing direct flights with only a stay-on-the-plane touchown in mainland Turkey. This should have had the effect of making Northern Cyprus a more desirable holiday destination but it had come too late and by the time regular direct flights had been set up, the effects of the oil price increase and the general economic recession had undone all the good work. Not that flights in and out of Ercan are at all convenient. Departure and arrival times at both Ercan and Stansted tend to be either very early in the morning or very late at night, so travellers from the UK to the TRNC must factor in either extra hotel accommodation or sleepless nights. And given that both airports are also a long expensive taxi drive from where most people live, it is not surprising that business had not been brisk.

But, maybe out of some counter-intuitive sense of optimism, it was also the year which saw the opening of Kyrenia's biggest, most lavish, most garish and most luxurious new hotel. The Savoy Hotel, on the main street through the town, opened its doors with only the merest murmur of publicity. Passing by it on the outside, one would have been forgiven for thinking that it was some kind of up-market place of worship or even the residence of a millionaire footballer or rock star. The whole external edifice is covered in intricately-carved marble tiles and the massive wooden main door would do credit to a royal castle. Inside, the luxury continued. The floors were exquisitely tiled with black and pink marble, on which lay large Chinese washed-silk rugs. The furnishings were equally expensive, the motif being 'sumptuous oriental' but done with such taste that the visitor was not overwhelmed by the effect. The pictures on the walls, although not of museum quality, were all by original artists.

There were bars, restaurants, a casino and shops and an escalator to transport you to a mezzanine where there was a pool surrounded by perfectly manicured gardens. Everywhere, immaculately uniformed staff were attentively on hand. As six—or seven—star hotels go, it lacked for very little.

Apart from customers that is. On the Sunday afternoon when we went to check it out, on one of our regular weekend jaunts, we noticed that there were almost no customers at all. The very few who were there were vastly outnumbered by the hotel staff. In the main dining room—the other restaurants of the hotel were closed—we were the only diners in a room with maybe 50 tables. There were several waiters standing by, some trying to look busy by refolding folded napkins, others just standing by. The silverware was good quality heavy silverplate and the napkins were heavy linen. A promising sign for me since one of my pet restaurant hates is paper serviettes.

So we should have been in for a good meal, in keeping with the ambience. Loydz chose a chicken sandwich and I opted for the only hot dish on the truncated menu.

"Steak?"

"No grills, Sir. Sorry."

"Seafood?"

"Sorry, Sir, we don't have it today."

"Pasta?"

"No pasta, Sir. Only this, Sir, ravioli alla pesto."

"So ravioli it is. Bring me ravioli and a glass of red wine."

Being the only diners, we expected a pretty fast service but here again we were disappointed. We could only assume that the chicken for Loydz' sandwich had still been alive and clucking when she had placed her order while my ravioli still had to be handwoven and flown in from Italy.

When the food finally did arrive, it did not taste too bad. Unfortunately the servings were meagre in the extreme. Personally, I do not like the sort of restaurant which serves a mountain of poor-quality food. I am not a big eater but I do need to have enough, which this decidedly was not, even for my modest appetite. This would be the first time in a year of Sunday trips to Kyrenian restaurants when we both agreed that we would need to take afternoon tea at a cake-shop and eat some calorie-busting cream cakes so that we could go home with enough food inside us.

What was The Savoy playing at? It was quite clear from our lunch fiasco that they are trying to turn away customers. Their business plan must have shown that there is no shortage of hotel accommodation in Northern Cyprus and several other casinos have that side of the trade pretty well sown up. Obviously they were losing money hand over fist. Unless that was the deliberate intention, of course.

In the early autumn of the previous year, the world's banking system had decided on mass suicide, mainly triggered by what was known as the 'sub-prime housing market" and aggravated by those Masters of the Universe at the banks, whose monumental greed would, no doubt, eventually be punished by their being given even more millions of dollars. I remember five to ten years ago when I was working for my old university with the American military connexion, just how often I would be invited to borrow half a million US dollars for repayments of just a few hundred a month. A moment's thought and a few seconds with a calculator soon showed up the implausibility of the offer. What made the whole bank implosion so incredible to me was why no one else ever did a little elementary arithmetic, especially those teenage *Wunderkinder* on Wall Street.

Still, it happened and it is little business of mine, except to make me wonder what to do with the small amounts I could save from my salary. We had, by this time got used to salaries being paid always six weeks in arrears although the official memos of the Institute would interpret this as 'two weeks in arrears' in preparation for their not paying you for the last two weeks of your termination notice. The best way to get around this, it was generally agreed, would be not to give formal notice but to take your month's leave from mid-August to mid-September. Then you could clear your bank accounts and get on the plane just after the euros had been paid in mid-September. This is, of course, not exactly gentlemanly but it does ensure that, even if you are foregoing half a month's salary then at least the half-month you are losing would have been when you were not actually working.

The other, contractually honest, option would be to hand in three months' notice according to contract but common opinion had it that if you did that you were just asking for trouble. As soon as they know you are leaving, they would stop paying you, or even worse, fire you on the spot.

Salary was always made through the Iktisat Bank, whose reliability record was a great unknown. But, given that some very big names had gone down in flames during the Great Banking Crisis of 2008, it gave pause for thought that we could turn up one day at the Iktisat Bank only to find that it had gone the way of Bear Stearns or Northern Rock and simply shut up shop, having invested all the Institute's money in loans on slum properties in Oklahoma. Not only would AIC have no money to pay us but anything we had been foolish enough to leave in the bank would have gone as well. The obvious thing to do, in a country whose currency had, only five years previously, been rebased by an eye-watering million to one, would be to withdraw all of one's salary in dependable euros the moment it had been paid and leave it in a sock under the bed so that one would always have the means, should the worst come to the worst and the Iktisat, the Institute or even the whole of the TRNC were to have gone bankrupt, to be able to buy, for cash, an airline ticket to escape.

I mentioned this to a Cypriot colleague.

"Oh, yes", she said, "that is what everyone does. You have to. All the faculty do it. Money here is just not safe."

Eleven

Another eventful week. The students had finally arrived back from their long break and ready to register. The time-table, the classes to be offered that term, is drawn up in advance and students could pick 'n' mix courses from a menu. This means that for each student, course selections must also be checked to see that they do not clash and that the student has the necessary background—the stipulated pre-requisite courses—to do the courses of their choice in the coming semester. This is tricky because every student has different requirements. The whole process of registering a single student can take up to two hours: especially if the student has some special requirements such as only wanting to take morning courses because they have an afternoon job or because they want to take the same courses as their friends. Students would return again and again to make small adjustments to their schedules. Quite often the same student would present him—or herself a dozen times over two or three days until they had got it completely right.

In an effort to try to bring order to this shambles, the AIC authorities had brought in some punitive measures such as putting a deadline on enrollment and fining late registrations. Fines made little difference to those students who could afford to drive around campus in the latest BMWs. And because all those late fees would be welcome to help raise the profitability of the business, putting a curb on late registration was actually counter to the spirit of the Institute's avaricious business model. So students could enroll for a semester more or less at any time during the term. It was not unusual for students still to be enrolling right up to the midterm exams or even beyond. There is a perverse logic in this. If a student wants to handicap himself by late registration, then we should let him do so because if he fails the course then his academic career will need to be extended at the cost, to him, of further tuition fees. I never actually saw a student register for a course and immediately proceed to take the final exam, but I can quite believe that it happens from time to time.

Registration was scheduled to take one week, but, in reality, it involved up to a month of continuous work. A queue of students would be waiting when I arrived at 9.00am and it would not be any shorter by the time I left at 5.00 pm. Each student would be shown the menu of courses open to them so that they could deliberate over their choices, rather as a millionaire diner at the Ritz would take his time choosing his meal while the waiter stood solicitously by waiting for instructions.

"Operating systems is hard?"

"Yes, quite difficult but you have to take it at some time."

"If hard, no take!"

And so it would go. Each student would need to be conducted through all the available classes until they had made their choices. The adviser would then need to handwrite the times and days of the courses so that the student could see if the schedule were convenient for him. A man of twenty-five or thirty, who might, in a more grown-up country, have already assumed the self-reliance and responsibilities of manhood, would leave the registration until he had consulted his male friends about which classes he was going to do so that they could be together in the classroom and, of course, arrange collaborative cheating strategies for the exams. The computer network used for registration was also prone to regular outages. All throughout the registration ordeal, the IT technicians would turn up from time to time to remove the cables from the laptop computers and registration would be halted.

"When will it be up again?"

"Maybe today. Maybe tomorrow. Who knows? This is Cyprus."

When a new faculty member, Turan, joined the team to teach computer programming, he was allocated his own share of students to register. Unfortunately, the personal laptop which the Insitute was to provide him with had not yet been delivered, so I took in my own machine and had it connected to the system so that Turan could use the laptop which the Institute had given to me. This arrangement only lasted two days, during which we were able to reduce the registration load by a good 2% or so. On returning to my office after a summons from the Rector, I found that an IT technician had gatecrashed my office and was searching my computer for viruses, or so he said. I keep a lot of personal material on my computer and I hate to think that he had copied some of it for his own amusement. (This is not as paranoid or far-fetched as it sounds—one of the vice-chancellors had once privately warned me that the IT department regularly checks the network to spy on faculty members.) The man from IT then told me that my machine was unsafe and I could not use it. Just to make the point, he took the cable away. So what could I do but to cancel registration for the day and hurry off home to enjoy the first stirrings of a terminal nervous breakdown?

Because TFC had not had the confidence to hire faculty members who were more knowledgeable about information systems than she was, which is a large and unexclusive group, she had staffed her classes with what few personal friends she had left. Indeed, she had been seen going around approaching teachers of English, tourism, chemistry etc. and offering them jobs as professors of information systems. Few had been willing to drink this particular poisoned chalice and submit themselves to her ill-tempered management style, so she had been forced to bring in outsiders, with who knows what qualifications. All these had to go as a first step and I did not renew any of their contracts. This left the MIS Department seriously shorthanded although getting rid of them did raise the intellectual level of the department. In fact, when term had started, it had been down only to Reban and me. Fortunately, I soon acquired Turan, a former senior lecturer from the Institute who was returning from his national service, which he had spent writing software for the Turkish Army. Another new faculty member was Celusk, an excellent network engineer with a CV to die for, who was brought in to teach data communications and software engineering as a part-time teacher. Not only were these two men both excellent teachers and information technologists, but they both possessed the primary qualification for the job i.e. they were both Turkish Cypriots.

This last was a vital job requirement because, just about this time, a directive came down from on high that no more foreigners were to be given employment in Northern Cyprus. Existing positions were reasonably safe, it was assumed, or at least safe until a local could be found to replace them, but new jobs were to be limited to those born within the island prison. Given that foreigners were essential if the Institute were ever to achieve its ambitions of international acceptability and given that there were simply not enough qualified locals to do the work anyway, the directive could only be construed as an act of either blind union protectionism, long since Thatchered away in the west, or simply mindless vindictive chauvinism. Either explanation is equally plausible or again, it could just be another way of saving money.

However, this new narrowmindedness did affect us directly. Loydz had finally got fed up with her housewifely duties and had come to a decision about her future career. She would work, she decided, towards becoming a primary school teacher.

Although she has a perfectly good degree in business administration, she was reluctant to return to that type of work. Since we had first arrived in Cyprus, the Institute had been stringing her along with promises of an office job, promises which were never, of course, anything more than cheap words. By this time, the penny had finally dropped that those empty promises were merely part of the inducement to keep me hanging on for the change of Rector so that I could take over TFC's job as Head of MIS and clean up the mess she had left behind. This new directive let the Head of Human Resources off the hook. It meant that she could go back on her word to Loydz with a valid excuse and a clear conscience.

To advance her career ambitions, Loydz had therefore applied to become a part-time unpaid teacher's assistant at the primary school which was attached to AIC. The primary school served as a feeder into the secondary school which itself fed into the sixth-form college which then fed into the Institute itself. All very efficient, not to say lucrative, since the fees were high. As the only provider of English-language—and British curriculum primary education in the whole of TRNC, it did have a very good reputation to go with its exclusivity, a reputation which was a tribute to its first class head teacher.

Loydz therefore went for an interview with the head who greeted Loydz with open arms-it is not often someone comes to offer you their services for free. Especially someone with all the requitiste personal qualities—intelligence, a maternal benevolence, excellent language skills etc. The job fit, one or two days a week helping a class teacher by, for example, sitting with young children just starting to read, was perfect and

Loydz left the meeting pleased with her warm welcome and happy to start her new career in primary education.

Two days later, the head phoned to withdraw the offer on the basis of the new ruling over the employment of non-Cypriots. Even, it appears, unpaid voluntary work was to come under the new proscription. One can just about understand the reasoning that places a cheap untalented Cypriot ahead of a well-qualified expensive foreigner. But even if one doesn't agree with those quasi-racist attitudes in this globalised world, to discriminate against a genuine helpful unpaid volunteer slops over into petty malice, an all-too-common attitude in that mean-spirited country.

We ran up against a couple of other similar examples of this low-level Cypriot double-dealing during registration week. The first was when I was still looking for a teacher to fill the last vacancy in my class staffing. I still needed someone to teach the infamous statistics class on Tuesday mornings. I had interviewed several people but none could do it, for some reason or another.

The same day, I wrote a reference for one of my excellent graduate students who was applying for a job at the Institute to teach basic computer studies to entry-level vocational students-a job he could do easily. He went to the interview and passed it with flying colours and, after a long discussion, he was offered the job. He went home, started to prepare his classes and bought some textbooks. The next day his job offer, just as it had been with Loydz, was withdrawn. This time there was no question of his racial qualifications—he is Turkish Cypriot to the core and fluently bilingual—but the job had been given to someone else better connected. He came to see me. I was surprised that he was not angrier than he had every right to be. But actually, he was quite fatalistic about the Institute's blatant double cross.

"That's how it's done here." was all he said.

That same day, I was phoned by the Head of the Chancellor's Office and was told that someone they knew needed some part-time work–"he has been promised a job". I told her that I just had this single slot for a statistics teacher.

"No, he can't do that. He's not qualified. Don't you have anything in computing?"

"Sorry, I"m all full."

And then she hit me with the clincher.

"But he is a close friend of Mehmet Bey."—the multimillionaire owner of the Institute.

Now, I recognise a direct order as quick as the next man, so that is how our statistics course came to be taught by someone with no knowledge of the subject and no experience of teaching.

To a naïve westerner, this casual breaking of a solid promise might appear unethical, even immoral. Which, to someone brought up to believe that one's word is one's bond, it certainly is. But the Turkish way of doing things carries with it its own fierce morality. A Turk has a very strong sense of right and wrong. It is just that he defines these terms differently. Where an Englishman would consider morality to be absolutes of right or wrong, the Turkish Cypriot sees this one-dimensional ethical position to be naively simple-minded. For him, right and wrong come not simple absolutes but as an infinite range of gradations depending on the persons involved and the closeness of one's social obligations to them.

It was now also that time of the year for the annual visit which Loydz and I had to make to the Muhtar and to the police to renew her residency papers, now that we were entering our second year in Cyprus. First, there was the obligatory trip to pay homage to the Muhtar at Cafe Squalid, where he traditionally held court to collect his tribute, which this year had been increased from 10 to 15 YTL. The usual papers—birth certificates, tenancy agreement, passports, copies of pages of passports in triplicate, marriage contract, plus copies in triplicate, copy of letter of husband's (mine) employment, postage stamps, photographs. This year there was no need for the blood-letting ceremony at the laboratory so she was spared that ordeal although she did still have to endure a particularly nasty olfactory experience at the court of King Muhtar. Then off to the police station for another supplication to the Cypriot money-gathering machine. Here the renewal fee was, at only 150 YTL (£70 or $120), surprisingly lower than the previous year's, but still a lot to pay for a rubber stamp from a civil servant in Lefkosa.

In addition to, and simultaneously during registration week, one was also expected to prepare and teach one's classes and, this week, to go to training courses laid on by a visiting American university who were anxious to make use the Institute for their own expansion plans. The idea was that we would enroll our students into their courses and to 'facilitate' their online operations by using our staff as unpaid teaching assistants to their regular distance learning faculty.

In an effort to become respectable, the Institute was particularly keen to develop its own international connections with various other institutions of so-called higher learning even if the co-operating partners were not exactly the cream of the world's universities. AIC may not have been bed with, say, Cambridge or the MIT, but they were more than welcome at Boggsville Community College or the Omaha Online University of Life's Experience.

These co-operative arrangements between disparate university-level institutions are very fashionable. They have a number of advantages for college presidents. For example, students can be milked for extra tuition fess when they travel between colleges. Senior managers can get in some foreign travel which makes them feel cosmopolitan and important and then there is the possible kudos which comes from projecting a low-level degree mill on to the world stage.

There is lots of educational tourism to be had. Cyprus is very popular with college principals and other senior education bureaucrats as a place to take a winter break at the expense of their home institution. What could be more agreeable during a winter term in England or one of the colder parts of the USA, than a few all-expenses-paid days in the warm Mediterranean sun with one's favourite mistress? Not that there isn't work to be done, of course. The contract of collaboration has to be signed, meetings have to be attended, predictable platitudes have to be vented, dinners at the best tourist restaurants have to be eaten and hands have to be shaken.

Nothing ever comes of all this effort, of course. The occasional student may be exchanged or the odd lecturer may find himself going to a summer conference, but on the whole, educational tourism is a junket-what the Americans call a boondoggle. If an ordinary teacher could ever catch a ride on the gravy train-seats on which are usually reserved only for the highly paid or the very highly paid-then it is no more than an occasional, once-in-a-lifetime perk as part compensation for their minimum wage faculty salary.

Ever since I had first come to North Cyprus, I had been unable to shake off the strange feeling that sometime in the last couple of years I died and gone to Hell and this is what Hell really looks like—a place where everything is run by Cypriots. The month-long ordeal of student registration did not have to be the nightmare it was at Kyrenia. Thousands of universities around the world manage to enroll their students quickly and with a minimum of fuss using desktop computers or temporary clerical help. No problem. But at the American Institute of Cyprus, they had somehow contrived to devise the very worst of all possible systems, not just for student registration but for all their systems. They were invariably clumsy, fault-ridden and user-antagonistic.

This was also the week when we were paid a proportion of our salaries in hard currency—six weeks in arrears. Naturally my modest €78 increase for my new duties as head of department had not been included, nor had I expected it to be, since the Institute did not believe in paying out a penny more than it was forced to. I had already accepted the extra responsibility and I was doing the job, so why pay me extra, even though they had promised it to me? What could be more wasteful than paying extra money to a foreigner?

When enrollments for Reban's class in database management had finally exceeded twice the capacity of the computer laboratory, we discussed dividing the class into two sections, He was reluctant, even though it should, he knew, carry a little extra much-needed overtime pay, something which, as a Cypriot national, he actually had some chance of getting.

"I'd like to do it, but will they pay me?"

"They should."

"No, even if you have a contract, they don't usually pay overtime."

"So why do it?"

"It makes perfect sense from the owner's point of view. A Catch-22. If a faculty member refuses to do overtime, the management will put sixty students in a classroom built for thirty. This will be difficult and uncomfortable. On the other hand, if the teacher makes their working conditions tolerable by dividing the class into two, then the work will be more congenial but they will be doing the second class for nothing."

"Isn't that just a little, er, immoral?"

"Oh yes, it's certainly immoral but only from our English point of view. Remember, this is Cyprus. Promises only count if they are made to a close friend or family. It's a matter of choice. Do you want a term of struggle because the working conditions are impossible or would you prefer to give up three hours a week making life easier for yourself?"

This grasping avaricious penny-pinching meanness was a striking feature of what was, in reality, a very rich institution indeed. Even the top management were not immune from its capricious management and this week saw the departure of one of the vice-rectors, a woman who had finally come to the end of her tether over unpaid extra work at weekends and evenings and the promised pay raises which never quite materialised. It never seemed to dawn on the owner of the AIC that the rapid turnover of staff was wasteful and costly in itself and that a relatively small investment in resources, faculty salaries, decent conditions and so on would bring untold dividends in academic standards, faculty work satisfaction, international recognition and by extension, higher students numbers and increased income. But the Cypriot way of thinking is that it is better to rip you off for a tenner now and gain your distrust rather than building an honest business relationship with you which brings them a pound a week for years to come.

But to see the Institute at its most dysfunctional, one would need to go no further than the shuttle bus service which was laid on for students and others to get them to and from the campus. The campus lay on the outskirts of the city about two miles from the centre where some of the dormitories were located. Supplying this free service runs directly counter to the fundamental ethos of the Institute, but it is impossible to walk the two miles between March and October because of the heat and there is no other transport available. Without the free shuttle bus, students would just not show up at all.

AIC ran a fleet of old buses bought second-hand from various German municipalites. Inside were notices in German about fare dodging and showing your bus pass to the driver. Included in these notices were very Teutonic commands about the numbers of sitting and standing passengers. No doubt the buses had been bought from Germany because not only would they have been serviced and maintained to the very highest Mercedes standards but also because the rules on passenger numbers would have been strictly enforced when they had been working urban transport in Stuttgart or Munich. But not here. Oh no, not here in Cyprus. They had come to the elephants' graveyard of motor vehicles.

The buses were scheduled to depart every hour on the hour to deliver students to and from their dormitories in various parts of the city. The bus would arrive at maybe five or ten minutes after the hour and the driver, who, to be fair, had probably driven two or three miles since his last rest and was therefore tired, would naturally be entitled to spend a little time smoking a cigarette or chatting up his little band of bus-driver groupies. Meanwhile, the students would be piling into the bus. The passenger limit were clearly stated—the total of *Stehfahrer* and *Sitzfahrer* together would be about a hundred, so naturally this translates, in Cypriot, into at least a hundred and fifty. During high summer, when the sun was at its most relentless, this number could be pushed up to at least two hundred. With no air-conditioning inside, the drivers would need to take longer over their smokes while the students inside were waiting, baking and melting. When the driver was ready and his groupies had been taken aboard inside the driver's cabin, the bus would proceed to kangaroo-hop its way down University Drive swerving from left to right around the 'sleeping policeman' traffic humps.

It was generally regarded as polite for the driver to stop and pick up extra passengers on the way—friends, family or just casual travellers who were hitching a lift. So polite and considerate were the drivers that sometimes they might have to stop and wait for ten or fifteen minutes for the wife or sister or the cousin of the driver to finish her shift at her job before getting a ride on the AIC bus.

The job of shuttle bus driver was clearly extremely arduous and once he had been trained on a route, the driver could not easily be transferred to a different one. If, for some reason, the driver was not available for a particular route, then that bus would not run and the students would have to make alternative plans to get back to their dorms.

Another feature of the system was that it would need different drivers for the outward and return journeys. It worked like this. Let us suppose that there was a scheduled bus going from the campus to, say, the Lyubianka Dormitory three miles away. One driver would be responsible for the journey from campus to Lyubianka and another would have the job of transporting students from Lyubianka to campus. This would mean that once the inward driver had dumped his load of students at campus he would then drive back empty to the Lyubianka Dormitory to await his next scheduled pick-up (plus 10 or 15 minutes or so smoke time, of course). Meanwhile, students waiting to go home to Lyubianka would be left watching an empty bus going back to their hall of residence and would need to wait until the driver whose job it was to drive the outward journey to show up. Naturally, I have made up the name 'Lyubianka'—no one would name a hall of residence after a KGB maximum security prison. No, the halls all had sensible names. For example, one of the women's dormitories was officially named 'The Gordon Bennett Hall', named, doubtless, by an Englishman with a sense of humour.

The shuttle bus management sounds all very unnecessarily wasteful and so it was. The empty bus pushing its way through a crowd of students to go back to where many of them wanted to go could very easily have taken them. But that misses the point about Cyprus. If the Institute employed the same man to carry passengers both ways, then some poor fellow would have to lose his job. The only, single, reason why there was any shuttle service at all was to provide employment for the drivers. And let us not forget that this was not an easy job—some of the drivers were making up to ten journeys a day, often covering at least thirty or forty miles.

The drivers did not like the students. No, that is an understatement. The drivers actually detested the students. When an empty bus drove past two hundred or so young people without stopping to pick them up even if they were going in the same direction where the bus could easily have taken them, many of the drivers could not avoid smiling a contemptuous smirk. Others had more direct methods of showing their dislike. For example, it was the practice of one of the drivers to put his foot on the accelerator as he approached the large crowd of students milling around in the road at the bus-stop. The students would jump away terrified before the bus would come to a juddering stop twenty yards or so down the drive. The effect was a bit like the bull run at Pamplona with, I am glad to say, fewer injuries, although I did see one poor fellow gored by the bus because he was not quite sharp enough to get out of the way in time. But it all adds a little amusing leavening to the bus driver's arduous life, does it not? And then they say that Cypriots have no sense of humour!

Why does the AIC management put on such a poor service for their fee-paying customers, you might wonder? Well, to start with there is no management of the bus service. The bus drivers manage themselves and they would be most put out if they were expected to report to a supervisor. So put out, indeed, that they would almost certainly down tools and stop work pending a grovelling apology from the owner/chancellor. The drivers union is very powerful and its Fred Kite's have influence right at the very top of TRNC society along with the hoodlums and the bent politicians. You would be forgiven for wondering why ordinary Cypriot citizens put up with such inefficiency and corruption? Why is there so very little public opposition to the inefficient and dishonest ways of the whole country? That question is easy to answer. Even if you are not actually feeding from the corruption trough yourself, then your spouse or your brother or your friend or your lover or your cousin certainly is.

"You've got to admire him, the owner of AIC. He's done really well—all those businesses. He's worth millions." I was told by one Cypriot.

"What's so admirable about what he does?" I countered.

"Oh you're just jealous because you don't have his money. He's a very great man."

So was Al Capone, I thought privately.

Another opening of another show. Today marked the start of the real academic year after the ordeal of registering students, an ordeal which would continue, on and off, for several weeks yet. But today, classes would be starting in the new academic year. And to celebrate, all classes were cancelled for the day so that the annual opening ceremonies could be held and to which all faculty were commanded to attend. In the morning there was a gathering of a thousand or so in the main hall.

Faculty were required to wear their full academic regalia. For men, this would mean sweltering in a robe over a dark suit in temperatures still up around 30C. There was little headway to be made by the limited airconditioning against the combined body heat of all those people. Women, especially those of a more uninhibited tendency, could cope with the heat problem more easily. The official AIC gown is a black affair made of heat-retaining polyester but it does have the benefit of a zip up the front. This classy attire is perfect camouflage for the woman who wants to stay cool by wearing only underwear or a bikini beneath the vestal polyester. It was widely rumoured that some of the more uninhibited women faculty members would even wear nothing at all under the black gown. But for men, no such relief from the heat was available.

Under the new rectorial regime, translations of proceedings into English were dropped and the entire ceremony was conducted in Turkish. It was, of course, difficult to stay awake during speeches by the Prime Minister, the Rector and someone else whose name and position I did not bother to take note of. Naturally I did not understand a single spoken word and yet I understood it all perfectly. Sententious platitudes by academic bureaucrats and self-important politicians are the same in all languages: all the listeners are required to do is to be there to clap politely. Not only could I have written the speeches myself, I am sure I could have written a computer program to write them.

After an excellent rendition of Django Reinhardt's '*Minor Swing*' by a duo of professional musicians, (Why do Turkish events always have French music, I wonder?) followed by a plangent dirge from a Turkish songstress, the torture was over and we were released for refreshments of coffee and cakes. Previous to my promotion, I would have not shown up at all, given that I still had the memory of my misery at having to attend the same ceremony the previous year. But this year I had little choice. Not only did I have to attend the morning session and clap the politicos but it was made clear that I was also expected at a second opening ceremony in the afternoon, being there now obligatory for someone of my new rank. I would much rather have been in front of the class my timetable indicated. Never has the thought of teaching computer operating systems seemed so much more enticing than what was on offer as a compulsory alternative.

Which was to be rounded up on to the Institute bus at one o'clock for a late afternoon march through the streets of the town. To start with, we all stood around outside the town hall for a couple of hours waiting for the procession to start. By this time the sun was well and truly up and my gown was generating its own internal nuclear heat. To add to the misery, we were standing only a few yards away from cafes selling ice cream and ice-cold beer to tourists wearing shorts.

One must applaud the immaculate timing of the organisers of this suffering. They seemed instinctively to be able to sense to the second just how long the victims could withstand it. It was just at the exact moment when I was on the point of screaming:

"Stop!! Stop!! In God's name, please, please, please stop and let me go!!! I'll tell you everything you want to know!!!" when the procession suddenly shuffled off, a disorganised rabble, down the 300 metres or so of Kyrenia High Street to the harbour, me feeling not only heat-exhausted but also self-conscious in my totally inappropriate academic robes. I expected not only jeers from the shoppers and passers-by but maybe even a few missiles of rotten fruit for my pretentiousness. A scarlet doctoral gown may look impressive on degree day at a British university, but outside, in the real-world, it is little more than preposterous fancy-dress.

The second ceremony consisted of yet more speeches, one, an exhortation to work hard, even in English! There was another playing of the Turkish national anthem—a pompous military piece reminiscent of the Toreador Song from Bizet's Carmen, some folk dancing and the laying of flowers on the monumental statue of Saint Kemal Ataturk. The whole farrago was rounded off by entertainment from a group of dancing girls from the arts faculty.

The dance was what one might call 'modern'—indeed the troupe reminded me very much of Pan's People who used to do similar dances on BBC television in the 60's and 70's. These six young women launched into a hip-swinging, arm-waving workout to the music of some excessively foul-mouthed American rapper. I think I can even remember all the words of the song. The first verse was simple. It went:

"Don't you s**t me, you ho, you motherf***ing ho."
"Don't you s**t me, you ho, you motherf***ing ho."
"Don't you s**t me, you ho, you motherf***ing ho."
"You f**k wid me, I kill you, you motherf***ing ho."

The next twelve verses? Same as the first.

The music had just reached the first, or maybe it was the second, *'motherf***ing'* before it suddenly went silent. We all thought it was because some senior AIC bigwig had pulled the plug in a fit of censorship. But no, it was merely a technical hitch and soon the vigorous sextet were back again to repeat the entire musical treat 'from the top' as they say in the music biz, banging it out at full volume until the very last swear word had been broadcast right across Kyrenia Harbour and as far as sound would travel across a crepuscular mill-pond-calm Mediterranean.

But all terrible things, and this day had been a truly terrible thing, must come to an end and, once the nubile sirens had dispersed, it did. We were given a final exhortation to study hard and, with a terminal benediction, the chains were taken off and we were set free. In my case, to the very nearest bar to quench my dehydration with delicious ice-cold beer.

There was, I heard, a saying that under the rule of the Sultans of Turkey a century or more ago, that a 'man's life hangs by a thread' so arbitrary and despotic was the absolute rule of the all-powerful monarchs and those who served them—their henchmen and lieutenants. Those times were swept away by Kemal Ataturk but something of the absolutist instincts remain in the folk memory. For example, the local management style is what one might call 'command and obey'. Higher ranking officers give orders to the lower-ranking for automatic obedience. There is none of the corporate consensus that you would find in a British or American college. In Kyrenia, faculty members are instructed in their duties with little or no consultation. A few formal committees exist such as the Senate and something called an Executive Council but they do nothing more than rubber stamp executive decisions already taken and add to them a superficial patina of democracy for the sake of the accreditation agencies.

It is difficult as a foreign member of staff to feel much sense of belonging to a cooperative enterprise where I had so little part, even as a head of department, in the organisational decision-making. This was certainly a common feeling among other expatriates I spoke to and I even felt it to be the same with my Cypriot colleagues. I was a mercenary with the means to be able to walk away at any time and therefore I was in a stronger position than some others who had committed their careers and their futures and even, in some cases, the futures of their families to the fortunes of the Institute. I often had to bite my tongue to stop myself pointing out to them the one-sided nature of corporate loyalty in the place.

A good example among many of AIC's attitude to its teachers was the lack of anything which might betoken a long-term economic relationship between employer and employee. Pension contributions and health care deductions and even income tax were unheard of. With the result that one's salary, which may or may not be paid on time, came as a gross sum, save for a nominal 1% withholding as insurance to cover the vagaries of the exchange rate of the New Turkish Lira.

Nor was it much different for the Cypriot teachers. Few of them in the Faculty of Business and Economics viewed themselves as career academics since for many of them, teaching for the Institute was a post-retirement pension supplement. This led them to take a fatalistic view of their long-term employment prospects and true to the folk memories of a people who might find themselves suddenly out of the Sultan's favour, the local teachers came and went at the owner's whim. It was a common occurrence to hear of someone suddenly disappearing in the middle of the term. There was never any announcement and the reasons were rarely even the subject of gossip. No, one day he would be teaching class and the next he would have gone.

"Mehmet's gone!"

"Mehmet? That old guy who was professor of architecture?"

"Yes, that Mehmet."

"But he was in class yesterday."

"I know. But he was called to see the Rector and then he was out."

"Just like that?"

"Just like that."

"Why?"

"No-one knows. Could be political."

Of course, a country where there are no employment laws and no concept of unfair dismissal, let alone anything like an industrial tribunal, might strike some employers as pretty much a Thatcherite nirvana. But it also has a downside to the employer which is that any notion of employee loyalty to the organisation does not exist either. If you can be fired on the spot for no reason at all, then simply getting on a plane when it gets too much, is the guilt-free option for the hired expatriate teacher. More to the point is that those with the least-replaceable skills and qualifications are the ones most likely to leave first.

But in the middle of this exhausting, depressing, gloomy week came the uplifting news that someone was interested in buying our empty house in Brittany. It was as if, in the middle of a long and uncomfortable sea voyage in the bilges of SS Cyprus, the clouds had suddenly parted and we had been awarded a glimpse of a distant sunlit land ahead.

Twelve

Once teaching actually started, life became a little less hectic. I was teaching four courses: my contract said three but the owner of the Institute needed every euro he could squeeze out of the students and faculty. I had two graduate classes in information systems and data networks plus my undergraduate course in operating systems. There was also a full course for the undergraduate fourth year projects to which a small group of politics students had somehow attached themselves, courtesy of one of my colleagues. Added to this were a sundry number of PhD and MBA students who are taking various tutorials under my supervision.

This would be a manageable load for a full professor in a normal university. After many years in the trade, he would have his lectures fully prepared and they would only require periodic updating. The rest of the time he could spend on academic activities such as research. As a subject expert, he would use his experience to develop his subject to the benefit of the university and the students.

That, at least, is the ideal. Not here. Here, after reaching the top of the tree by achieving the rank of full professor, he would find himself doing mainly what is fancifully called 'administration'. This is, of course, a universal complaint of professors everywhere—that they are repeatedly taken away from scholastic work to do various management and administrative tasks such as writing reports, applying for grants, meeting external examiners, developing links with local industry, reviewing PhD theses and so on. In most universities, the price of promotion to full professor entails taking on a great deal of this kind of work and I was fully prepared for it.

Unfortunately, what passes for necessary professorial administration elsewhere is not the same kind of administration a professor will find himself doing in Kyrenia where 'administration' means elementary clerical work of the sort which could easily be done by a junior clerk e.g. classroom allocation, student enrollment, data entry of grades on both paper and computer, filling up of forms on behalf of students too poor in English to understand the instructions, checking the transcripts of graduating students which would then need to be re-checked by the registrar's clerical assistant to whom he would be answerable and the signing, collating and reporting of summer internship reports. All, of course, in triplicate in both paper and electronic formats.

After forty years in academia, I felt that my life had come full circle, as if I were a living embodiment of some esoteric eastern belief system here we live our lives on a continuous moving belt which brings us around to our original starting point before we are allowed to get off. So, as a result of all my strivings for greater prestige and seniority, I was awarded, not with commensurate responsibilities and the professional respect which goes with them, but with a return to the sort of elementary entry-level work I might have been doing as a sixteen year old school leaver.

This feeling of circular regression was brought home to me particularly acutely by a nine o'clock visit of the new Rector to my office. A few months previously the Institute's general secretary had, before his demotion, designed a scheme requiring all faculty members to swipe their cards on entering the building, so that their attendance could be timed. Now, this scheme had failed for a variety of reasons such as the fact that, as usual, the Institute's lines of communication meant that many faculty had not been informed about it and that not all faculty had been given ID cards. Even many of those faculty who did have cards and who knew of the scheme could not be bothered to cooperate with it. When the system stopped working after a few days because of a technical failure, it was quietly abandoned.

Naturally, a scheme to monitor and thereby control the comings and goings of teachers would be the sort of idea which might appeal to someone who would be insecure enough to need to buy his degree. Especially someone from a culture which equates rank, not with maturity and responsibility, but with a fancy title and the automatic right to unquestioned obedience. So after the ignominious collapse of his swipe-card idea, he arranged for the new Rector to check up personally on the attendance of faculty by a series of spot checks. Naturally, she would be required to obey him. While she would be the nominal CEO of the organisation, and, what is more, a mere woman, he was the man with the actual power. So on his command, she started a program of visiting faculty offices to check who was in and who was not in for the contracted nine-to-five. Several colleagues, many of them putting in a regular fifty or sixty hour week, subsequently received tart little memos warning them about their 'time-keeping'. One recipient of such was an assistant professor, a retired diplomat known for working in his office every evening up until ten or ten-thirty at night and who was devoting most of his waking hours to academic endeavours on behalf of the American Institute of Cyprus.

I did not get a letter myself but I would happily have joined a protest by those who did, had they chosen to confront the situation. Instead they merely joked about it and waited to see if the Institute authorities would be taking the matter further, or just letting it drop. Calling the general secretary's bluff, as it were.

This incident brought home to me yet once again the feeling of having been time-warped to an earlier stage in my life and career. I realised that the last time I had been required to stamp a clock card had been forty-seven years previously when, as a nineteen year old, I had worked in a factory in Manchester. Then I had found the whole experience of such tight control over an employee's time and freedom to be both counter-productive, because it encouraged people to skive off real work, and also deeply humiliating. I resolved then that I would never in my life work as an hourly-paid wage slave, a resolution which kept me going through college and graduate school, fuelling my ambition to become a university teacher where, I had seen, the teachers might be poor but at least they did not have to jump when the foreman said jump.

The reason why so many talented people choose to become university academics is because they are willing to make this very trade of personal and professional freedom in exchange for minimal financial security. There are many clever people in universities who could make more money outside: very many of my colleagues have possessed very tradeable skills indeed. It is, however, usually their personal choice that money is not everything and selling one's freedom to work and study at one's own pace and in one's own time in exchange for a bigger wage packet is, at best, a dubious Faustian deal. So when a bureaucrat, especially one who is deep-down jealous of the freedoms enjoyed by academics and who is undoubtedly conscious of not having any earned academic rank, attempts to impose the attitudes of the factory on to hard-working and serious lecturers, one's hackles are naturally raised. It was, most university teachers will tell you, precisely to get away from such attitudes that they came into the job in the first place.

The irony is that rigid working hours will, very quickly, reduce rather than improve academic productivity. The resentment caused by forcing professors to work to rule will mean that the usual working week of 50 to 60 hours will be reduced to just the prescribed 35 hours in the office and the organisation will suffer as a result.

There was to be a commemoration the following Monday of the seventieth anniversary of the death of Kemal Ataturk, the founder of modern Turkey. It would take the form of speeches and the reading of poems in the Main Hall. There will be playing of the Turkish national anthem, laying of flowers and a minute's silence. All must attend.

The idolatrous worship of Ataturk so long after his death, is a weird feature of life in the TRNC. His picture and his statue are everywhere. His likeness features on the coins, on the stamps and on the banknotes. Statues of the great man, often poorly-sculpted monumental bronzes many times life-size, can be found in every school and workplace. Walls are decorated with his face in *bas-relief* and great plaques record his sayings. The Institute itself has many depictions of him—as well as the tons of bronze, there are huge badly-executed portraits to be found on any free space.

This is perhaps not so surprising given that Ataturk remains the only famous Turk that anyone has ever heard of. Even little Belgium is supposed to have had up to six famous people. But in the last hundred years, Turkey has only produced just the one. So it is not so strange that the Turkish people have made a cult of his worship. The anniversaries of Ataturk's birth, his ascent to power and his death are all celebrated by national holidays. To criticise him, even academically as a historian, is a blasphemy punishable by fine or imprisonment or, for foreigners, deportation. So his (Should that be 'His'?) importance as an iconic figure far exceeds that of any other religious leader or prophet in quasi-secular modern Turkey.

In Turkey and the TRNC, unlike in some other Islamic countries, one is able to get away with being an atheist or a Christian but not to believe in the divinity of the Blessed Ataturk would be a criminal heresy. To an Englishman, this is more than just strange, it borders on the surreal.

In Britain, we make little fuss of our national heroes, maybe because we a have so many of them. Our world-class heroes—Shakespeare, Churchill, Newton *et al*—do not have national days. Their anniversaries pass without notice. Maybe if we had to make do with just the one, say Horatio Nelson, then maybe our bank holidays would fall on the anniversaries of his birthday, the day he lost his arm, the Battle of Trafalgar and maybe even the day he first seduced Lady Hamilton.

By two months into the autumn term, the number of new students had fallen off. In one week just before midterm, I enrolled maybe as few as six or seven. The computer system was no longer listing the names of all paying students so we faculty were sent a memo exhorting us to create class lists so that the registrar could try to reconcile them with the list on the computer. At least that is what I think it said, given that it was written in a kind of Turkified pidgin English

Why they bothered us with the task of compiling interim class lists at this time in the term was something of a puzzle. Although the student registration computer system had already closed down for new student enrollments, the boys and girls of registration were still taking tuition fees over the counter and then sending the new student to a faculty 'adviser' whose duty it was to find classes for them. Most classes had long since been filled to overflowing, but any student arriving with his three and half thousand euros is not going to be turned away now, is he? The computer did not record these manual transactions which is why faculty had to produce those real class lists, the production of which had been one of the reasons why the computer had been installed in the first place. That is not to say that there were no rules about late registrations and class attendance. There were many. There was a rule, for example, that a student could not pass a course with less than 75% classroom attendance. Then there was the rule that late registrations would incur a 10 euro daily fee. (Which was about to be raised to a sliding scale of €25 or €50 by order of the Executive Council i.e the owner.) One would have to agree that it is vital that any seat of learning should have rules and these rules should be written down quite clearly on the syllabi and on the registration forms. Not necessarily implemented, of course, but definitely written down.

This flexible, relaxed attitude of the administrators to their own rules had not gone unnoticed by the studentry who would constantly seek ingenious ways to take advantage of it. A student appeared at my door.

"Can I help you?"

"I wan' thees class".

"Which class?"

"Thees class. 'Operating Seestem.'"

"Are you registered for it?"

"No. I have no money."

"I am teaching it this term. Wednesday evenings. Six pm. Room LR1"

"Teacher, you no unnerstan'. I already pass Operting Seestem but my grade, eet ees not good."

"Why do you want to take it again."

"I need better grade so I can get diploma."

"Then take my class."

"No, teacher. Then I have to pay. I have no money."

"So you have a problem."

"Teacher, what you can do ees let me come to you class an' I take exam."

"But that is not possible. I could not record a new grade without you being registered."

"No, teacher, you don' unnerstan'. I take special exam from you. No register. You change grade for me."

"I can't do that."

Naturally I have abbreviated the conversation, since it always took several repetitions of each sentence before any sort of mutual intelligibility could be established. But it was clear that he was expecting me to name a bribe price. This might be a usual way of doing things and I was aware of the techniques of opening a dialogue for negotiation. As I expected, after being turned down by me, he then went to Reban and tried it out on him. Reban came to my office straight afterwards.

"What are we going to do about him?"

"No problem. He wants a better grade and there are always empty seats in the evening classes. He can go and register for the course like any other student."

He would, of course, be back. The student searching for a bribable professor returns day after day in the hope that the professor will have relented and taken pity on him or will have been charmed. (Yes, they really do think they are charming!) Or maybe the teacher will just be sick of the sight of him and will do anything to get rid of him. Not me though. I have never taken money for favours from a student in my life and in this finale of my career, I am not about to break my duck now. If this particular young man fails to get his diploma because he did not study 'Operating Seestem' properly, then he can always write BSc(Failed) on his business cards. That or he can continue paying his fees and retaking the course until he gets a good enough grade to raise his grade point average to a diploma-passing level.

Another big event at the start of term was the election of a student representative to the Board of the Faculty of Business and Economics. It had been an initiative of the incoming Rector to add student representatives to the various committees. A revolutionary idea. Or at least it was revolutionary when it was first tried out in western universities after the student uprisings of the late sixties. So the Rector told the deans to get on with it and the Dean told me to find a suitable student for the role of representative for MIS.

I think I was expected to point to a likely face and say

"You ! Yes, you there! You, you're it."

That would be the sort of electoral process which goes down well in this part of the world. When a bright young woman called Gamze put herself forward for the job, I thought that would be enough. No such luck.

The undergraduate MIS Society had kindly invited me to its first general meeting of the academic year, something from which I had been excluded when TFC was still head of department. At the end of the meeting, the society's president, the very articulate, intelligent and bilingual Mehmet, invited me to say a few words and I told the students about the new arrangement for student participation on the Faculty Board after which Gamze made a speech in Turkish which seemed to suit most of the audience. Just as Mehmet was about to close the meeting, another student asked to be allowed to address it. This was Samson, a first class student from Nigeria, who made a very fluent off-the-cuff speech about the democratic principle and suggesting that it might be better if MIS students were to be allowed a choice, especially a choice between a local, Turkish, speaker and an 'international'. Samson was chosen as the second candidate and I was given the task of arranging an election.

No one had ever done democracy before in the Faculty of Business and Economics so there were no rules about how to run an election. So I invented a procedure which I thought would be fair. First, I announced by a notice on my office door that candidatures would be accepted until the end of the week and that voting would take place between Monday and Friday of the following week. When nominations had closed, leaving Gamze and Samson as the only candidates, I printed ballot papers and constructed a ballot box. To ensure fairness and avoid multiple voting, I invented the rule that students who wished to vote would need to present their student ID cards to receive a ballot paper.

All went well until the Wednesday of voting week when Reban came in to tell me that some students had objected to the ballot box being inside my room. My room is not exactly a closed sanctuary—students barge in and out of it all day. It would be nice to have a quiet study but the Institute is not exactly a haven of scholarly calm such as might be the atmosphere at an Oxbridge college. In this more mundane environment, one opens the door to one student and two or three others crowd in uninvited. So what was their complaint, I wondered? That I was not being impartial? That I was going to falsify the count? This suspicion of dishonesty would be a natural reaction, of course, and totally in keeping with the suspicious cultures of both the AIC and the TRNC in general. They need not have worried because I was totally indifferent to the outcome. My role had been simply to create a fair democratic procedure in the absence of an existing one.

But clearly something had upset the Dean and the Faculty Secretary. Most likely it was the fear that I, as an international, would somehow pervert the election in favour of a fellow international. This is a fearful paranoid culture where all foreigners are resented or mistrusted. Unless they are being fleeced, of course.

The next thing that happened was that the Faculty Secretary burst into my office in a flaming temper, and began accusing me of a number of crimes such as not consulting her before holding an election, not following the proper rules (which did not exist), of taking too long over the voting and other things which, frankly, just passed over my head. Her wild hysterical outburst brought forth the Dean, who told me I was doing the election all wrong and in his train came the assistant to the Secretary and a phalanx of students attracted by her screams.

I returned their anger and told the assembled throng that, yes, they could stuff their election and here are the box, the papers and the list of ID numbers of students who had already voted.

The Dean pronounced. We will, he said, complete the election this evening at the start of the Wednesday evening class i.e. my fourth year class on Operating Systems. This had the effect of disenfranchising any student not actually attending a Wednesday evening class i.e. most of the students in the department. Moreover, it ensured that, because my class was composed almost entirely of Turkish students, then Samson, who had been hoping to muster his vote on the Thursday, would be seriously disadvantaged. After this antidemocratic pronouncement, the Dean departed, showing his contempt for this particular international by a dramatic slamming of my office door.

But all's well that ends well, in this travesty of democracy. The Secretary and the Dean got the result they had demanded—an overhelming vote for the Turkish lady, who, to be fair, had been quite happy to accept my *ad hoc* electoral rules. And Samson was gracious at being cheated out of a fair chance.

The main thing was that the winner was Turkish. The intervention by the Secretary had come just in time. If the Secretary and the Dean had not acted so decisively, then who knows, one of the internationals might possibly have got the seat on the Faculty Board. And not only does the loser not speak any Turkish, but he is, horror of horrors, black!

The week of the election had not been a good week except that it hardened our resolve to leave Northern Cyprus at the very first opportunity and such an opportunity did indeed arrive just as we were at our lowest. Loydz puts it down to the power of prayer and her regular appeals to divine intervention do indeed succeed often enough to confound an old hardened sceptic like me. So, completely out of the blue, there came a very firm offer of a temporary job in Bulgaria at 50% more salary than I was getting in Cyprus. The job would be pretty much what I have always done i.e. teaching computing and information systems to students studying under the American educational system but with none of the hassle of being head of department.

That bit of good news, that my name had been selected by some celestial escape committee, alleviated an otherwise literally painful Monday, when I had to have Botox injections round my eyes to alleviate my chronic blepharospasm, a troublesome complaint in which the eyelids blink involuntarily. The effect of the Botox is to weaken the muscle cells and thereby inhibit the involuntary distonia. Each treatment lasts for about three months before it needs doing again. Mehmet the Neurologist, who was to perform this procedure, was not a man to be put off by a little pain, especially if the pain was to be endured by the patient. In fact, the whole process, which, when I had had it done previously, had been relatively painless, was, this time, excruciating.

I wonder why it is that some medical doctors take a delight in the inflicting of unnecessary pain when they could quite easily use various painkiller drugs to make the experience less uncomfortable for the patient? I have two theories. The first is that many medical practitioners, while not being exactly closet sadists, have a detached, even scientific, interest in the way pain can subjugate a patient. The second theory is that, in the simple slogan, if it isn't hurting it isn't working. It may just be that, this being Cyprus and the fee for the procedure being at least three times what I would pay elsewhere, the patient might therefore expect a little pain as a guarantee that the job had been done properly.

I took the next day off as a justified sick day while I contemplated the residual discomfort and the two black eyes which I had now acquired. We, Loydz and I, discussed the Bulgarian job offer at length and it was agreed that we should go. The problem, as always, would be Loydz' entry visa and the international conspiracy to make it as difficult as possible for Filipinas to move from country to country. I emailed my contact in Bulgaria with the problem. No, problem, he returned, if she has an EU visa already then she can come into Bulgaria. This, of course, was exactly what the Director of Human Resources at AIC had told us two years previously, before the incident of being turned away at Frankfurt Airport. One lesson I have learned in life is never to believe anyone who begins a sentence with "No problem . . .". So we checked the websites and emailed the Bulgarian Embassy in Nicosia and, yes, there could well be a problem and the solution may have to be for her to go back to Manila to get a visa from the Bulgarian Embassy there! What the website did not mention was that there is no Bulgarian Embassy in Manila—it had been closed as a cost-cutting exercise. Any Filipino wanting to visit Bulgaria will need first to get a multiple entry-visa to Japan, Vietnam or Thailand and present their application to enter Bulgaria at one of the Bulgarian embassies in Tokyo, Hanoi or Bangkok.

One wonders what sort of inhuman bureaucrat makes up these kinds of rules. They have neither logic nor compassion but they are mindlessly applied by immigration policemen everywhere. Not only must one have the right piece of paper, but it must have been given to you in the right part of the world. There is never any flexibility of judgement. The immigration police at the airport have the power to grant entry, as we had discovered. One would have thought that they should be allowed the discretion to let pass a middle aged woman with her husband who were in possession of all those same documents which would have needed to be presented at the embassy six thousand miles away !

What makes the system even more ridiculous is that if one does actually have all the right papers with all the right stamps, issued by the right office on the other side of the world, then one can turn up at the airport in the full dress uniform of an Al Qaeda car bomber and waltz right through immigration without a problem.

Thirteen

The visa problem was on hold until we could organise a face-to-face interview with the Bulgarian Embassy in Nicosia. Meanwhile, other news from AIC further attenuated my affection for my current employer. Having taken a day off sick to nurse my battered eyes, I went to the office of Human Resources to tell them why I had not been there, just in case they were going to penalise me, or even remove me from the payroll altogether. Why, I asked her when I was there, had my small, paltry pay raise of €78, for being head of department, not been paid with my September salary on October 16th?

"Yes," the HR Director explained, "we are rescheduling all salaries. Your raise has been held back. All raises will be paid as a lump sum in six months time. And we are also going to change the way we pay regular salaries so that different proportions are now going to be paid at the beginning and the middle of the month."

As I was leaving the HR office, one of the secretaries tool me aside and told me the good news that there was an as yet-unannounced plan to cut all faculty and staff salaries by 10% across the board.

When an organisation starts to fiddle around with salary payments, it is usually a sign that it is in financial trouble. But how? The Institute had recently increased its numbers by about 20% to something well north of five thousand and very many of those students were handing over €5000 a semester or more for tuition and other things. One does not need to be an accountant to see the disparity between income and outgoings. A student report from a meeting with her, that the Rector was worried about finances, confirmed my suspicion that something was wrong. But how, just how could all that money just disappear?

Other little meanesses showed up in the same week. The first was a memo from the top concerning the upcoming holiday or bayram, in two weeks time. The holiday is traditionally over four days, Monday through Thursday, and Friday is supposed to be a normal working day. Why open for just one day, when, in most well-run organisations, it would be more cost-effective to shut for the whole week? Students of the Institute would all be going home to Turkey to spend the entire week, including both weekends, with their families, so no one would be in classes on the Friday. So why insist that faculty be available for just the one day? And why make it official via a memo threatening disciplinary action against any faculty member who does not report for work on that Friday, whether they had scheduled classes to teach or not?

For myself, I had already bought air tickets for a trip to the house in France which had to be cleared for the sale and I had been intending to cancel my classes on that day anyway so that we could do the job properly over a full ten days. Since I had no intention of changing my plans and losing the thousand pounds or so already committed to the trip, I decided to defy the order. Since the Institute would be obliged to discipline, possibly even fire me, then clearly some sort of showdown was approaching. Better to go and take a 'what the hell' position than try to comply with this arbitrary *diktat*. So we made the decision that we would leave Cyprus at the end of January whether we could get the visas for Bulgaria or not. The only thing we could not agree on is whether to tell the Institute in advance and thereby risk the possibility that they would stop paying me my salary as soon as I had resigned or just to go ahead and so only lose my final month's pay.

Because what was certain that both an honourable resignation or a moonlight flit would cost me money. The only calculation was how much and how to minimise the loss. Loydz was for the latter course but I wondered if it might be better to give them a chance to act properly. In what were obviously straitened financial circumstances for them, saving my salary would be something they would be very happy about. As a full professor, I was earning one of the top salaries in the Institute, even though it was only about that of a London traffic warden and which did not go very far in a country where the prices for most everyday items were what they might charge in Bond Street.

So, I reasoned, the whole business of arranging the holiday not to include the Friday and then issuing the official warning was a deliberate provocation. Anyone not obeying the order would be fired or would lose pay. Either result would be what the management had planned for in their cost-cutting. Since, I reasoned further, there could be no question about our trip to France, then a preemptive resignation and the thought of their not having to pay me after the end of term might just forestall a punitive loss of salary in the meantime.

One reason why organisations plead poverty is usually part of a classic policy of fattening it up for sale. In this case, the huge increase of student numbers plus a ruthless program of faculty dismissals combined with petty revenue-generating and cost-trimming schemes follows the standard pattern for an organisation which is about to go under the hammer. The question is, why would the owner want to dispose of such a profitable money-making machine? A difficult question, but these things take time and there are persistent rumours, or fears, that the long-standing Cyprus

Problem i.e. the partition of the island, might actually soon get resolved. Bringing the Turkish Republic of Nothern Cyprus back into the European fold would be a relief for many but a disaster for some. This illegal country had been a godsend to freebooters of all nationalities, many of whom would have little to look forward to after reunification apart from difficult interviews with various regulatory authorities. Or, in some cases, a period of confinement to permit them to contemplate their life choices.

Ideally, AIC would have liked to get along without any of those expensive teachers at all, but if they did that, even the most inattentive student might notice. So it was necessary to keep a minimum of lecturers on the strength, preferably the lowest paid. Extra paying students can always be stuffed into the corner of a class. Indeed, classroom accommodation in the Institute is rather like the banking system—it only fails if everyone uses it at the same time. In fact, student classroom attendances were always around 70-80% of signed-up students so it was quite safe to run classes at 25% over classroom capacity, knowing that at least a fifth of the students would not show.

The Institute could not be faulted for its ingenuity in coming up with money-saving or money-making schemes. One of the more bizarre was a new ruling, as usual never formally communicated but passed on like Chinese whispers, that faculty must only order food from within the campus. This rule, which had been created on the hoof, only came to light when a woman teacher ordered a takeaway pizza from the town to be delivered to her office. Within minutes, she got a call back from the Rectorate telling her that she was not allowed to order in food from outside on pain of dismissal. The problem was not the buying of food from the town but that she had been ordering her takeaway from the wrong establishment, since the owner also had an evening job as proprietor of a number of catering outfits in the town centre. (Sorry, patisseries.)

At the same time, another ruling was leaked out that faculty and students must do all their photocopying on AIC premises and must not patronise the many other Kyrenian copyshops which were in direct competition with the AIC. Since illicit photocopying makes up such a large component of the economic activity of the country, and probably brings in even more money than take-away pizzas, this was a serious step. I ignored the command and gleefully did all my essential photocopying at a place in town owned by one of my graduate students. I was becoming what the English call 'demob-happy'—light-headed at the prospect of early release.

What makes the pizza incident so typically sinister is that it came hot on the heels of a memo from the Institute's general secretary to the effect that people had been discovered using the internal phone system to make personal calls. It came as little surprise to learn that one's phone calls would be monitored. I had been warned a long time before, by one of the vice-chancellors, that one's emails would be routinely read. Better, he had told me, to use one of the many Internet cafes for emailing and only ever communicate by personal cellphone. Although one wonders, in this sort of paranoid setup, whether the owner might also have some connection to the local cellphone provider in order to track one's personal calls as well.

It was just about this time that the Institute came up with another of its fancy schemes. The Best of Both Worlds scheme, known as BBW, had been hurriedly installed after the collapse, for reasons best not even alluded to, of the AIC's relationship with The Virginian University. The connection between AIC and VU had been some kind of marriage of convenience. It had certainly not been about the money. There were only about 50 VU students on campus, studying the same courses as regular AIC students. There was a secretary, a vice-chancellor in charge of it and a couple of teachers dedicated to this little outgrowth of Washington DC in an alien foreign clime. But it must have been an important relationship, because its breakdown caused a desperate panic to find a new partner to maintain an American connection.

What had happened between Kyrenia and Virginia never became clear, except that there had been a bitter and acrimonious parting of the ways amid allegations of financial hanky-panky on both sides. Details were scarce but what gossip did come out was both squalidly disreputable and totally believable.

So there was a hastily conceived replacement plan and what it amounted to was a suuposedly attractive package within which undergraduate students would be able to study for a regular degree from The American Institute of Cyprus, added to which they would be able to pick up a second degree from its new partner, the Northern American University, a distance education online college with offices in the American midwest. The idea was that the students would take a number of American courses online in addition to their normal classes. What AIC was signing up for was a deal in which both degrees, one from AIC and one from Northern American, would be offered to the students at the same price as before. Which, sounds, in theory at least, a pretty good deal. BOGOF—buy one, get one free!!

Faculty members were dragooned into these hastily conceived BBW plans and from their number a project manager was appointed at the start of term with instructions to get the scheme up and running by, er, the start of term. The senior management, having defined the strategy to her, then rubbed their hands, told her to get on with it and then went back to being senior managers, doing what senior managers do best i.e. management organisational charts, mission statements, important meetings and giving orders. One or two of the press-ganged lecturers realised that this would be a lot of extra work for no extra pay since there would be no extra revenue flowing to the Institute. Indeed some actually had the temerity to ask the very obvious pointed question—why? Why indeed? The 'idea', if such a hare-brained scheme can be dignified as an idea, was that AIC faculty members would act as unpaid assistants to regular paid American online lecturers. The classes would be taken online by AIC students and local lecturers and professors would give tutorials, grade assignments and supervise exams for those Cypriot students on the scheme. Ever the Jeremiah, I could foresee a number of problems with the scheme, lecturer motivation, more work for no extra pay, being not the least of them.

The initial intake of students involved would be a pilot group of about 200 but within a year, the grand plan ordained, all the students of the entire Faculty of Business and Economics would be studying for the BBW and, shortly after that, every single AIC student would be working on both degrees. This was where my very acute sense of *déjà vu* cut in. Ever since I can remember, I have heard senior people in universities putting up schemes and plans and sometimes just plain scams, to cash in on the online, distance learning market. With a single teacher at a computer terminal and hundreds of thousands of fee-paying students out there receiving online 'tuition', the cost benefits are obvious. The blue sky is for the money men and the bureaucrats who run education these days—online means fewer teachers, no classrooms, no expensive libraries, no student services etc. etc. Just bang together some canned courses, get yourself a website and bingo—we're in the money!

It looks like a real winner, and to be fair, it does have some advantages for those students who just cannot afford to go to college full time. In fact, every university in the world is trying to tap into that market of students living in locations remote from a college or those single parents who cannot get child care while they attend evening class. The market is completely saturated and not just with those marginal institutions from academia's fourth division like AIC. Even Oxford University, a brandname synonymous with academic quality and integrity, has its own Department of Continuing Education where students can work on their own at home for much of the time, with the promise of a week under the gleaming spires once a term.

But Oxford is Oxford and the Ameican Institute of Cyprus is not exactly in the same league. I have no doubt that Oxford can fill its online courses with good quality students at whatever fee level they care to set. What is more, one could be sure that those triple-A schools would be sure to get the online teaching format right, something which is much harder than it looks. In spite of what the average penny-pinching academic bureaucrat would like to believe, a profitable distance learning program needs more than an overloaded Internet server, a student-designed website and fearful faculty willing to write their lecture notes as web pages for free. The problems of doing distance learning successfully are not at all obvious to someone who is neither a teacher nor information technologist. A proper distance learning operation just cannot be done on the sort of etiolated shoestring available at AIC.

To start with, the technology is expensive and needs to be reliable, which means wide band-width servers with automatic backup when for when things go wrong which they certainly will from time to time. It also means 24-hour technical support, given that most universities see distance education as a way of tapping into a world market. In addition, the website needs to be designed to a high professional standard which is also expensive and it needs to be connected to an optimising search engine which will present the casual net surfer with the university's name on the first page of millions and that doesn't come cheap either.

Although this would not bother the suits from the Rectorate Building on the hill, distance education is also very hard on the teachers. An online distance class takes roughly about three times as much effort as the equivalent live face-to-face class in a classroom. On-line teachers will need to spend more time at their computers than they ever would spend in class, since students expect a round-the-clock service. As a result, teachers of online classes will need to be online for several hours a day, every day. Distance education is also expensive in terms of academic material. Classroom notes can be written and refined to last several years but online material gets used up very quickly, especially in technical subjects like mathematics where class examples cannot be used more than once.

There are plenty of ambitious ideas about virtual classrooms with video conferencing or videoed classes on demand but although the technology for these is available, it is still beyond the budgets and expertise of your average university IT department. The load, or bandwidth, required for simultaneous transmission of hundreds of streams of on-demand web pages or video clips, is enormous and certainly beyond the ability of most universities to provide. Especially on the sort of pared-down budget most of them allocate to this kind of grand plan. Even if it were possible to put all those ambitious ideas into effect and all the students were also able to receive streaming video, the class presentation could not be done by the teachers themselves—it needs proper, professional, studio production.

There is also a simple-minded belief that there is a large untapped third-world market for American online education. This is false as well. Even the dimmest corrupt third world dictator has enough sense to realise that cheap mass university education is the cheapest, most cost-effective way to stimulate economic growth. There are very few developing countries these days which do not have an affordable English-language public university system of their own.

The faculty member who drew the short straw to get the scheme up and running was a part-time Dutch woman called Saskia and Saskia good-humouredly set about the herculean task of setting it all up in a matter of weeks. Soon she was in my office, getting my opinion. I was in conference at the time with one of my graduate students and the three of us discussed the huge size of the problem which she had just been awarded. One of these was the glacial slowness and the unreliability of the existing network servers and the fact that the Institute's Internet service was being provided by a cost-effective Internet Sevice Provider in Beirut. Obviously, it was Silicon Valley, Beirut, but definitely Beirut. Not a good start. So I passed her on to our main man, Celusk, who had a reputation for having done wonders with networks in both very prestigious and very difficult places.

Celusk was a brilliant network engineer who had been taken on at the start of term to teach classes in computer networks and software engineering. He soon proved himself to be a man of great talent and ferocious energy—just as his glittering CV had promised. So much so that he was regularly offered work in other departments such as aviation—he had studied at a well-known aeronautical university—and with "Best of Both Worlds". As well as teaching he was also attempting to start work as a graduate student in the MBA and PhD programs in MIS.

Soon Celusk was reporting back to me that some progress was being made to find ways to circumvent the labyrinthine excessive network security which had been installed in the Institute's system by a fearful IT manager who was most reluctant to let anyone into what he considered to be his own personal system. But Celusk, being a real-live expert, was slowly unravelling its mysteries. But, as he reported to me, he would need to be with the system over a period of time before he could entrust it to a non-professional. So he went to the AIC general secretary and presented his bill for work done so far with an outline plan of what future work would need to be done before the Institute's new distance education system could be made functional.

No dice, was the official response, you are a part-time teacher here which means that this network management is part of your duties as a lecturer. Celusk had his response ready.

"Look," he said, "I am not asking for cash, but I am willing to do the job in exchange for the €2000 tuition fees it will cost me to register for a graduate course each term."

"Sorry, we can't even do that!"

"This is not," he told me, "the way they did it at Harvard."

No, but that's the way they do it here. This is Cyprus.

For Loydz and me, the week began promisingly with a trip to Nicosia to visit the Bulgarian Embassy. The American University in Bulgaria was anxious for me to start work and the contract was awaiting me, pending a resolution of the usual problem i.e. how to get a visa for Loydz given her status as an international Filipina pariah.

The Embassy was situated in a pleasant leafy suburb in Nicosia. The weather was gently warm and all around the orange and lemon trees were in full fruit. We had arrived early—Erkal's taxi took us to the United Nations Green line separating the two halves of the island and then we steeled ourselves for the interrogation by the Greek Cypriot immigration police which, for once, did not happen: the young policeman who examined our passports was charm itself and, after a cursory look at our marriage contract, he let us into the European Union. A quick taxi ride later and we were second or third in line at the Bulgarian Embassy.

Naturally, a visa was not granted on the spot. The efficient polyglot young woman on the front desk soon recognised the enormous problems of letting a Filipina accompany her husband on a short stay visa. It would be difficult, blah de blah, need to refer to Sofia, blah de blah . . . Something we have become used to. We know we will get the required permissions in the end because we always go prepared with full documentation. This includes birth certificates, passports with residency stamps, marriage certificate, employment details, job offer letter, tenancy contract of current residence, title deeds of house in the EU, details of residence in the new country, bank statements from banks in three countries, utility bills and so on.

The natural instinct of the jobsworth bureaucrat is automatic refusal. They are like Mr. Micawber in reverse—always waiting for something to turn down. Every consulate or embassy has s slightly different list of what documents they require from the applicant and the scrutinising official will always look carefully through all your documents in a desperate search to prove that you are missing one or more of the essential papers. What is on the required list is never published and changes regularly, so one must always carry every piece of paper they could ever need for every trip. If a document from their private list is not in the thick folder you have brought with you, then he (or she—vindictive officiousness is not sexist) will seize on the missing item to administer the *coup de grace*.

"Aha!!" he/she will utter with climactic triumph,

"You do not have . . ." and they would name the one single document which you had not realised you had needed.

"You must go back to our embassy in your own country. Apply visa there!"

We had become used to these tricks and Loydz has amassed a thick folder of everything they could possibly need to know about us. If they need to see details of the maiden name, date of birth and birthplace of my mother, we can show them. If they need to know when and how much was my last electricity bill, the information is there. What about our municipal tax bill from five years ago? Sure thing—got you covered! Indeed, full biographical details of both of our sets of parents (mine long, long dead) are now part of the state database of many a foreign country. Carrying this personal mini-encyclopedia is a vital part of one's armoury in the bitter struggle against the malign black forces of the world's immigration bureaucracy.

While having all this information at one's fingertips is a necessary condition for success in the battle, it is certainly not a sufficient one. The border guardians can still surprise you. One of the requirements which the Bulgarian consulate demanded and which we had not thought of, was to see our air tickets for the trip to Bulgaria, something we had never had to provide in advance before. Now this is a very smart and beautiful move in the chess game. No airline will let you on their planes without a visa for your country of destination and if the embassy will not give you a visa without a ticket you would need to lay out a large sum of money for the ticket on the off chance of getting a visa to go with it. In reality, it does not make one jot of financial sense to buy an expensive air ticket in advance until you have the stamp in your passport.

Actually, this brilliant Catch-22 looks like a winning checkmate by the immigration people and for many players it would be. But there is a strong countermove which will keep the game open and that is calmly to ask for a meeting with the consul himself i.e. to go up the management chain. It helps if you are well-dressed so that you appear respectable, and also that you speak confidently and politely. Looking and sounding like a bum off the street will get you nowhere except back out on the street. So you must keep calm and stay polite and watch the mental cogwheels turn around in the counter clerk's official brain. It is not her job to spark off an international incident by turning down someone who looks important, so she will refer you to her boss, the consul, who will certainly hear you out properly. He, of course, will be fully aware of the air ticket trick but he also knows that you know that he knows that it is just a device for getting unwanted riff-raff off the embassy premises.

So, without committing himself, the Bulgarian Consul reviewed our case symapthetically and asked us to bring back more papers such as correspondence from the host confirming the job offer and the name of the hotel where they would put us up temporarily when we arrived, both of which we would be able to supply.

We did also mention that we would not be buying air tickets without a visa and he just smiled.

This being exam week, I was called upon once again to invigilate exams in other departments, including a one-hour stint neatly timed for mid-afternoon Saturday, which effectively ruined the whole day. During the long boring hours I had already spent pacing around a classroom looking out for the exam cheats, I wondered, not for the first time, how I could not see any evidence of what was, I had been told, a veritable epidemic of cheating and copying. But student ingenuity was such that I was completely fooled. I never once saw anyone copying from another student or copying from a smuggled-in cribsheet. However did they do it, I wondered?

I don't think I was the only one taken in. My fellow invigilators would occasionally move a student from one seat to another for whispering to the person at the next desk but whatever was going on below the surface never came within view of my own invigilational periscope.

The evening class in operating systems had had to be relocated and retimed because room-scheduling was now a process which was centralised under the control of the Vice-Rector for Operations, new in from Turkey. At the same time, it was also independently devolved to the various faculty secretaries. A very AIC way of doing things. For the first week of term, forty or so students had showed up in a computer laboratory meant for thirty.

I had immediately gone to the very top i.e. the faculty secretary, to get the room changed. The only slot left in a room big enough for forty students had been on Wednesday evening. So all term I had been teaching the fundamentals of operating systems to a varying group of maybe thirty and forty students comprising a core of real students out to do some learning and a straggling band of peripatetics, who came when they felt like it. Because of the irrationality of the registration system-half badly written computer program and half badly managed manual system, the exact class personnel was a complete unknown and unknowable, quantity.

Which was all fine and standard procedure, except that come the midterm exam, which, unusually, I was to invigilate myself in my own class time, a total of sixty-eight students arrived to take it. I had allowed for some leeway and had printed fifty exam papers but I found that I needed to send Turan, my co-invigilator, back to the photocopier for eighteen extras as more and more unknown faces came in through the door.

The next day I was visited by three students from the core group of regular attenders with complaints about the high level of cheating which had gone on. I, of course, had seen nothing. I could put that down to my ageing eyesight and my other optical problems but Turan, a sharp young man with untrammelled vision good enough for recent military service, had seen nothing either. The students were astonished.

"But they all cheating!! All of them!!!"

"How? Who?"

"They were copying from each other! They were talking!"

"But I saw nothing."

Which was the truth—just how do they work this trick?

"You must do something! Stop them!!"

"What would you like me to do?"

"You not give good grades to cheats. And cheats not be in class"

"I agree and if someone has obviously cheated on a question, I will not give him any marks for it. But tell me, where do all those extra students come from?"

"Some, they come in to do exam for friends. We not see them before. They borrow ID. Some register and not come class because night. What you do?"

I explained to them some simple facts of academic life.

This is the classic dilemma. A professor, even a head of department, has a responsibility to make sure the exams are run fairly for all the students. Unfortunately, this responsibility does not come with the authority to do anything about it.

A professor might expel a student from his class for exam cheating or for any other anti-social offence but he would soon find himself in serious trouble if he did. The student's appeal would certainly be upheld and the professor could well find himself on the wrong end of disciplinary action. Since the Institute is aware of the existence of extensive exam fraud but takes no action against it, then the alternative hypothesis must hold that AIC welcomes it. The students know this and use the information to avoid studying for the exam, relying instead on getting through with a little help from their friends. The whole thing is really an elaborate game. The students pretend that they do not cheat and the authorities pretend to believe them. And as long as both sides keep to the rules of this game, both sides can continue in business—the students can slowly get their diplomas and the Institute can quickly get its money.

There is a wonderful exchange in Tom Sharpe's brilliant satire of a corrupt Cambridge college, 'Porterhouse Blue', where the Master, played with brilliant effect by the late Ian Richardson in the TV version, expostulates to the Bursar

". . . but's that's tantamount to selling degrees!"

"No, Master", comes the response, "not tantamount, identical!"

Especially true in Cyprus.

A new obligation in my exalted status as head of department was my required attendance at what is pretentiously named The Executive Council of the AIC. Naturally, it has no executive authority at all, in spite of its name, nor, for that matter is it a council—'a body to manage the affairs of . . .', to quote the Oxford English Dictionary. The Institute is a long way from being a democracy but to satisfy the accreditation authorities, who, in effect, give the owner of the Institute his licence to print money, lip-service must be paid to the quaint notion of decision-making by committee.

I was not looking forward to a pleasant morning even though the previous meeting, a month before, had been short, if not especially sweet. But by now, I surmised, correctly as it turned out, that the new Rector would be getting into her stride and would have much more to say. My experience of her management style was that she tended not to appreciate the difference between consensual decision-taking and mere empty talking. She had, she told us at her first meeting, some background in counselling and psychotherapy where problems are 'talked out'. A worrying sign, I thought at the time. Personally I have never understood the need to let the congenitally garrulous waffle away without being cut off. If there is more than one of them in the group then each will try to outdo the other in tedious long-windedness, competing desperately to have the last word. It may be considered good manners in polite society not to interrupt when someone is talking but what is polite to the wafflers is most definitely impolite to the captive audience who have to endure them.

To run a meeting effectively, these people need to be slapped down by curtly cutting them off when the less loquacious members of the committee start yawning. Running a meeting full of time-wasting prima-donnas, as many academics tend to be, is a skill requiring firmness, even brutality, to stop the whole meeting degenerating into an empty talking shop. These, unfortunately, are not the skills of a 'talk it through' counsellor/psychotherapist, which meant that a meeting which could have been wrapped up in thirty minutes was dragged out to a full three hours as two sufferers from extreme competitive verbal diarrhoea were allowed to babble on unchecked.

As it was, the agenda for the meeting was short, with only four simple items and the decisions following from them had already been taken. The meeting began in English, there being two English speakers present, myself and the Vice-Chancellor for International Affairs, who was present in his temporary role as Dean of the Law Faculty, a role which he assumed every time one of the regular deans of law took a vacation and decided that anything, even unemployment, would be better than the frustrations of teaching European Law to monoglot Turks. Soon, though, the committee members lapsed into Turkish and, after my fellow English speaker had left the meeting, was conducted almost entirely in Turkish, with just the occasional aside from the Rector, who would tell me what was going on. As the token international, I was just window dressing, there to help keep up some kind of false front that administration is not limited just to locals. But for what purpose? This was, to all intents a Turkish university, so why pretend otherwise by empty gestures like including a foreign national on its committees?

Indeed, only in one part of the rest of the meeting was English used and that was when a statement of policy on paying for overseas academic trips was debated. It was presented by the Rector and she clearly expected it to be accepted on the nod. The six-point statement was not exactly written in the very best Churchillian English. Indeed, it contained several amusing grammatical and spelling errors. But it got the message across, so I felt it was not too bad as a piece of written English and I would have been quite content to let the Rector have her way. Unfortunately, one of the two verbal incontinents insisted that we go through the piece line-by-line. This was obviously a ploy so that he could show off his skills in English to his fellow deans.

"This part here say, 'No teacher to not get expenses more one or two times in year' is wrong. I give correct. It should write 'Not teacher to get expenses more two time in year'. That is better."

Oh dear, oh dear. This masterpiece from the theatre of embarrassment went on for a good forty minutes as my mood moved from amused to near-suicidal. Once the dean who had taken on this proof-reading task had finished lecturing the assembled company on the rules for the placing of participles and prepositions in English sentences and after he had impressed the meeting with his several neologisms and misspellings, the policy statement, which had started out in understandable but broken English, had been rendered well-nigh incomprehensible. I have to say that I kept my mouth tightly shut throughout. Not only do I not want to be held even partially responsible for such a public fiasco but, by not being asked my opinion on English phrasing and sentence construction, I was being deliberately made aware of the redundancy of my role as the token Englishman. A redundancy which I interpreted to mean that I would never again be needed at one of their 'Executive Council' meetings.

I could not join in the rest of the proceedings because they were entirely in Turkish and no votes were taken because the decisions had already been made. So all I could do was just to sit still and be quiet, as Miss Kershaw, my very first primary school teacher in 1946, had frequently told me to.

But during the first part of the meeting, while the Executive Council had still been using English, it did throw up some snippets of information to yield interesting glimpses into the thought processes of the senior management. The first was from the Registrar who was explaining a decision we would shortly be rubber-stamping i.e. one to try to regulate the termly registration shambles. The solution was not to be the necessary reorganisation of the whole system with properly thought-out and working computer programs. No, the solution would be much simpler—a draconian set of much higher fines for late enrollments. The Registrar also told us that even though the computer system had been switched off weeks ago, students were still enrolling even as the midterm exams were taking place.

So, she informed us, the fee for late registration would be increased to €25 a day for students who registered up to a week late and to €50 a day for students who enrolled later than that. I could not resist asking an impertinent question. If, I asked with as much *faux-naïveté* as I could summon up, a student who was, say a hundred days late, could he pay his fees and the hundred days' late enrollment fine of €5,000 and just take the final exam? And is there any final cutoff date, after which all enrollment ceases for the term? I got my answer in the form of a faint pitying smile. No, the smile said tacitly, money is money—any student who can bring enough cash to the registration office at whatever time of the term will be made very welcome.

The final discussion was a long furious argument in Turkish which had to be explained to me. Apparently, one of the assistant professors in the Department of Computing was seeking a promotion to the rank of associate professor. There would need to be a promotion interview board including two local academics and two external full professors. The big debate was on how to pay for the costs of bringing two fellows from Ankara and Istanbul. The regulations of the Turkish Ministry of Education made it clear that the home institution of the external professor would pick up the bill. That seems fair to me. Over a period of time, the expenditure will balance out across all the participating schools. It is generally regarded as a mark of prestige for a university to be supplying external interviewers just as it is a distinction for the interviewers themselves. But the discussion raged on about whether these regulations also apply to Turkish universities in Cyprus, and, if they do not, who would foot the bill? At the end of the discussion the Rector reported the conclusion in English for my benefit. What would happen, she said, would be that the assistant professor himself would be paying for his own interview costs. So what would happen, I asked, if he had to pay out all this money and did not pass the promotion board. Just too bad, was the reply.

Ah well, it is not just us internationals who finish up screwed and demotivated. They do it to each other as well. For myself, I never quite understood why the poor fellow would want a promotion anyway. It's not as if he would be paid any more.

Fourteen

Monday Decmber 1ˢᵗ 2008 would be the crunch time. After a weekend of deliberation, I wrote out my resignation letter. The reason for deliberation was on the wisdom of actually informing the Institute first and defying received wisdom that it is better just to leave suddenly without notice. I would shortly be putting conventional wisdom to the test.

Since I would be doing the quick contract in Bulgaria starting February 1ˢᵗ, I figured that the Institute might notice if I were not present for the dreaded spring registration beginning on February 8ᵗʰ and they would feel even more justification for not paying me the mid-February pay. Pay which had been earned during the very strenuous January exam period. I was helped to my decision by a useful piece of information supplied by one of my Cypriot informants who let it slip that the owner/chancellor of the Institute was also a resident of the United Kingdom and owned property in Kent, England. This made up my mind for me. My strategy would be to play it straight and if, as would be quite likely, my January salary did not appear in February, then I would be able to sue him in the British Small Claims Court. So, in a spirit of publish and be damned, I wrote a formal resignation letter and gave it to Human Resources, reflecting *en passant,* that while honesty may indeed be the best policy, then dishonesty

---

225

is, at the very least, the second best. I was, after all, betting a month's pay on my guess.

To load the dice slightly, I did not tell Human Resources that I was going on to a new school for a fast-in-fast-out hired-gun contract. That would certainly have made their minds up for them. Instead I pleaded ill-health and age, factors which were certainly valid in my case, since that was also the day I had to return to the sadistic Mehmet the Neurologist for a follow-up on his Botox injections. 'I want to retire because I am old, I am tired and my eyes are going,' certainly has a more sympathetic ring than 'I'm off to where they are going to pay me properly.' Doctor Mehmet, ophthamologist, neurologist, cosmetician and butcher, did, incidentally, declare himself satisfied with his handiwork so I was spared further pain at his hands. I did think of telling him that his treatment hadn't actually worked and my condition was no different than it had been before I had paid him a thousand YTL. But I was in no mood to allow him further experimentation on me-better to endure the blepharospasm than to submit to further torture at his hands.

The next day, we made a round trip into Kyrenia to pay our rent and check that the December salary had been paid. The appearance of salary in my account, even a day or two late, as it customarily was, would always give me a small *frisson* of surprise and excitement. Tales abounded of arbitrary non-payment and when the salaries did actually appear, a buzz of grapevine gossip would zip around the faculty. "We've been paid!" professors and lecturers would whisper to each other in tones of barely-suppressed astonishment.

At the bank we met GD, a former German diplomat on a second post-retirement career in the groves of academe.

"Another thirteen yesterday" he said.

"Thirteen?"

"Yes, thirteen fired."

"My God! Who?"

"Mainly people we haven't heard of. I've put a notice on my door—'Enjoy the day—it may be your last'."

Could this really be true, that the new Rector was turning into Vlad the Impaler? If the purge was proceeding at a rate not seen since the autocratic reign of Comrade Stalin then no-one could be safe. I lost no time in consulting a Cypriot informant I had been cultivating as having insider knowledge at the highest level. I called him my 'snout'.

"It's true," he confirmed, "twenty went yesterday and they are looking to get rid of a lot more. Maybe another hundred."

"Who?"

"Well, the general secretary is not popular with the new Rector so it has finally been confirmed that he has been given a job teaching business here in this faculty. Didn't you see Cemaliye running around fixing up his new office? She and the owner and the general secretary are part of the in-crowd. Remember how long it took you to get an office? Well, it's who you know, not what you know."

"So who else is out?"

"Quite a few-some have been here for years and really need the job. The head of the primary school was demoted to classroom teacher."

The head of the primary school ! How could they? I had met her and like everyone who meets her, I had been very impressed. The school was especially successful. In only four years, she had turned it into one of the best schools in Northern Cyprus. Following a rigourous English curriculum but with an emphasis on bilingual teaching, the school had moved up to first choice for both local and expatriate parents. This success was entirely down to the drive, professionalism and energy of its head. More to the point, from the perspective of the owner, the head was generating fees and hence profits like a money-printing machine.

So why demote such a prize? Perversity perhaps, or maybe some personality clash between two strong women? Or possibly, and more plausibly, simple racism. The new government-sponsored policy of removing foreigners and replacing them with locals could be the entire reason. The new Rector had been appointed from Ankara for some political purpose which was only slowly becoming clear. But if she could overrule the power of the owner/chancellor, she would need to have powerful friends indeed, and they would almost certainly be in the the upper reaches of the Cypriot or even the Turkish Governments. It was also becoming clear that she was on a short-term mission and she would only be Rector until the job of turkifying the Institute was finished. Whatever the reason for humiliating the excellent headmistress, no responsible organisation, especially one so passionately committed to the noble ideal of short-sighted greed, would be so stupid to neuter one of its most productive golden geese. But then, the unfortunate headmistress was lacking the most basic qualification for employment-she was not a Turkish Cypriot.

A couple of days later, I received a visit from the Director of Human Resources. She made all the right noises about how my going would be a loss to the blah, blah . . . and how the students all liked me, blah, blah . . . etc. etc. All standard HR guff.

I told her that I was retiring on health grounds blah . . . blah, that I had had a very enjoyable experience, lots of good friends blah . . . blah . . . etc. etc. All standard reply-to-HR guff. After the formalities, I cut straight to the chase.

"So what is going on?"

"It's very difficult. A lot more people are going to be leaving. I can't say anymore but there are going to be a lot of changes."

"OK, so what about salary? I haven't been paid the extra 78 euros a month for being head of department as it says in the contract."

"That's also very difficult. That extra will be paid, but as a lump sum in six or nine months time. We are also reorganising the schedule for salary payments, but I can't say anything about that now."

"Obviously I am not going to be around to pick up my bonus"

"No, but we would like to pay it to you if you were staying."

"So, what else is new?"

"I can tell you this and don't quote me. There is going to be an across-the-board pay cut for everyone, faculty, office staff, the lot."

"A pay cut! That should really bring a smile to a few faculty faces!"

"I know, it's not good. But we really don't want to lose you. You"ve done a good job here and the students like you."

"Thank you. But, let's face it, you haven't exactly done much to motivate me."

"Yes, I know that Chris, and I"m sorry."

"I"m sorry too, but I"m afraid sorry won't quite cut it. A pay cut is just another way of telling me to get lost."

Other things started to happen around the Institute. First we noticed that the student coffee bar had been closed. Loydz and I would often use it to get a quick coffee before evening class when the other refreshment stops had all closed for the night. It was to be, someone told me, a cake shop. (Sorry, patisserie.)

Well, yes, one could see the logic of that. The owner was, first and foremost, a caterer who owned a chain of patisseries and coffee bars right across the TRNC. His second profession was that of car salesman and he was the proud owner of a number of vehicle franchises. Indeed he was one of the leading suppliers of motorcycles in the whole of Cyprus. So what better than to bring all three of his business interests together—why not use his own university to sell his cakes and motorcycles? Which makes perfect sense—a cakeshop on campus with a row of motor cycles for sale in the forecourt! Brilliant—just what higher education ought to be about!

I have long believed in the principle of synchronicity. That is that when two things happen at the same time, then they are, in some way, related, even if the connexion is not immediately obvious. Often one can only make sense of seemingly unconnected events by virtue of their simultaneity. Thus it was that a whole slew of seemingly unrelated happenings were taking place at the same time—the firings, the pay cut, the building of the cake shop, the motorbikes, the sudden change of our American academic partner plus a weird little directive from on high requiring all faculty to clear our doors of any notices attached to them. With no working communications such as an adequate number of notice boards, most faculty would stick notices to their office doors to inform students of minor things such as the name of the person in the office, the dates and times of the exams or the location of classes. All these *ad hoc* notices had to be removed, we were ordered by Cemaliye. Even the residual marks of the sticky tape were to be completely cleaned off. Why, we asked her?

"The Chancellor does not like to see paper stuck to doors. He is bringing a very important guest."

"Who?"

"The American Consul from Nicosia."

So it was we scrubbed down our office doors and the elevated pair of VIPs made their tour of inspection. What was it for, this American connection? Things were certainly getting curiouser and curiouser.

The pattern was starting to emerge. The new policy would be that only Cypriots need apply to work there. Where they would find a cadre of universiy lecturers and professors of the required calibre from the limited pool of Turkish Cypriots was a question I left unspoken. But the fact remained that the Institute appeared to be on course to replace all the internationals with Turks or, better still, Turkish Cypriots. Applying my synchronicity theory, I also noticed that reunification of the Greek and Turkish halves of the island was back on the geopolitical agenda. Perhaps this process of turkification was a panic measure to stuff the Institute personnel with Turkish Cypriots while they could? Once the TRNC was back inside Europe, EU rules on labour mobility make it illegal to discriminate against fellow Europeans. Given the shortage of qualified teachers on the island and add to that the fact that faculty salaries would very likely rise after reunification, the Institute could well find itself very attractive to non-Cypriot professors and lecturers who would, by virtue of their internationally-recognised degrees and superior qualifications, displace the locals. If there were going to be any discrimination towards locals and against foreigners, far better to get it over with sooner rather than later, before the EU put a stop to it.

I met my snout at The CafeDaD. My conversations with him were rather like the discussions with Deep Throat in Bernstein and Woodward's *All the President's Men*. Direct questions were out but he would confirm or correct my suppositions by terse replies and occasional illuminating asides. He was, I had learned, very well connected, with contacts right at the top of the Turkish Cypriot hierarchy.

"Tell me if I have it right. The AIC is being fattened up for sale?"

"That's right."

"Why? It's such a money spinner. You don't have to be a professor of accountancy to work out how much profit it's making."

"Correct, and all in juicy euros."

"Let's see. He takes in all those tuition fees in hard euros and pays most of his bills in soft YTL?"

"Of course. Be stupid not to."

"So the YTL from all his businesses get transformed into euros which he can put into a British bank account on the Greek side?"

"Naturally."

"And now he's sweetening the balance sheet—20% more students and firing staff."

"That's about it, yes."

"Anybody interested?"

"Of course. Turks, a Turkish consortium, Israelis, could be several."

"Price about 80 million euros?" (I estimated a business is worth about ten times its annual profits.)

"A bit more than that."

"A hundred mil?"

"Spot on!"

"Why now?"

"Well, he has financial problems."

"Financial problems with a goldmine like this?"

"Yes, he's a bit overextended and now he needs every penny."

"So he's increased canteen prices, got rid of anyone he can, he's selling his motorbikes on campus?"

"Yes, but he's a bit behind with his tax and social security."

"How behind?"

"Let's just say four years. Do you remember Bengu, who used to be here in HR?"

"Sure.",

Bengu was the HR Director when we were first misled over the question of entry visas.

"Well, Bengu is now working in the States but she had to make a special trip back to Cyprus to chase up her missing social security. He hasn't been paying it."

"But when North Cyprus becomes part of the EU again, the boys in Brussels will be asking questions."

"Precisely."

"What about the American connexion?

"You mean the spies, Rick and Dick?"

"I didn't say that."

"No, but spies will do. They do spend a lot of time at their embassies in Nicosia."

"Ok, your word—spies."

"If it goes to the Israelis they will bring in their own people."

"How do you know all this?"

"I was born here—I know people."

I was in conversation with him when who should walk in but the Mayor, The very same Mayor who had been helpful the year before during the great shit-in-the-street episode. He greeted my snout like a favourite son and, seeing my connexion, he greeted me warmly for the first time. No more the curt nod—this was the full hail-fellow-well-met—a strong handshake, a grip on the arm, full eye contact, the works. What it is to have important friends.

"He's up for re-election. His party may not get in so he needs the votes." said the snout.

"In fact the whole government is likely to be kicked out. This is bad news for The Fat Chemist, who will probably lose her job as well."

He then went on to tell me that TFC had found herself another job at a nearby college through her connexions as a cousin of the prime minister who would, popular opinion had it, not survive the next election. As is normal in most of the world's democracies and semi-democracies, the paying and repaying of favours and obligations is the main currency of statecraft which also has, as its corollary, the natural process of looking after one's friends and extracting retribution from one's enemies. As the old political maxim goes—in defeat bitterness—in victory, revenge. And never was this universal process so openly apparent than under the azure skies of this out-of-focus paradise.

"Yes," smiled my snout, "one more year and she will be out."

Amen to that, thought I.

My resignation letter was in. I had expected some reaction but it was slow in coming. The Dean of Business and Economics, a harrassed man, did come to see me and asked me if it was true that I would be leaving.

"I hear from the Rectorate Building that you are leaving?"

"Yes," and I gave him my prepared speech about my failing eyesight. He made no attempt to pretend that my leaving would cause him any regrets.

Sorry, I said, but yes, my eyes were now giving me so much trouble that it was not possible to continue. Which was at least partially true especially after Doctor Mehmet had worked his magic on them. When I mentioned that, in addition to my ophthalmological problems, I had had to have an operation for an enlarged prostate, his eyes widened in sympathy.

"Ah, yes" he said, with a sigh of understanding. For men over sixty, the shared endurance of troublesome prostates and hernias is a masonic handshake, effortlessly bypassing culture and language.

"Can you suggest anyone we could appoint for next semester?"

It so happened that I had a couple of good CVs available and I handed them over.

"Are they Cypriot?"

"One is, one isn't"

I later heard that he had run the CV of the Cypriot past Reban who had approved it.

We still, even at the end of our stay in Cyprus, had a continuation of the accommodation problems which had dogged us from day one. It was now getting cold and the apartment, which we were renting from a British couple, was only really comfortable during the warm months. It was fairly newly built and clearly it had been intended as a summer home. This became obvious as the sun got lower in the sky and the night-time temperatures fell to British lows. The lack of insulation made it unpleasantly cold at the bottom of the year, although we did our best with electric fan heaters and extra blankets. The main problem was that the solar panels, admirable for their 'green' environmental political correctness, were no longer able to supply hot water for the shower. There were numerous switches, two of which were both labelled 'Heat immerser. Switch off after use'.

We followed these instructions to the letter and endured several days of cold showers before the plumbers came around to sort out the problem. Which was, they told us, that the apartment had never before been lived in during the winter. As a result, the plumbing had never been fully tested. Over two or three visits they were able to track down a number of build-quality defects in the water supply system such as hot and cold pipes being connected to the wrong taps, the heating switches being mislabelled, the seals around the baths and showers not being waterproofed and the immersion heater not being connected at all. Small negligible defects in the Cypriot building code of practice.

Another feature of Cypriot life is the constant round of holidays or bayram's as they are known. They come thick and fast, and no month goes by without at least one day off. During the fall semester from October to January and notionally covering fourteen weeks, I saw some classes no more than eight or nine times. There were breaks for the Muslim holidays such as the big week off at the end of Ramadan and a week at the beginning of December for the Hadj. For both of these weeks, the holiday would spill out into the two adjoining weeks so that one could be sure of no more than 50% attendance even when the Institute was officially not on bayram. Students would go home to Turkey for a full two weeks knowing that an indulgent AIC would not impose any sanction for non-attendance and that their grades would be unaffected because the exams were always taken as a group effort.

In addition to the Muslim observances, the Institute also recognised a regular succession of political holidays commemorating various Turkish and Turkish Cypriot events such as independence days, national days, the anniversaries of important events in the life of the Blessed Ataturk and other sundry celebrations. For a few days before these holidays, the twin flags of Turkish Cyprus (A red crescent on a white field with two red stripes) and Turkey (A white crescent on a red field.) would be displayed in all profusion. Mind you, they were profuse enough on ordinary days-including being displayed prominently year-round on the mountain tops.

The AIC also celebrated some western holidays including Christmas Day. Officially, this had been ignored the previous year, but the coming of the new Rector had led to a relaxation of the rules and all the students, Christians, Muslims, Hindus, whatever, gleefully took full advantage.

Then there were holidays with no particular religious or political significance such as New Year's Eve and New Year's Day—both were taken. And then there were various secular celebrations to mark the opening of buildings or the start of term.

There was also a two-week break in the middle of the term for midterm exams and another two weeks at the end of term for finals. I did ask myself the obvious question of how the students were expected to learn if they were spending half the term off the premises, but then chided myself for my naivety. What learning?

The bayram was also a time when small Cypriot children could learn the streetwise ways of their elders and use the holiday as a chance to extract cash from the foreigners. It was, Reban told me, the practice to give children money at the bayram. And with so many bayrams, it was clearly a regular little earner for junior extortionists to learn the age-old Cypriot craft of parting an Englishman from his money. In our first apartment, when we had been guests of the unlamented Mr. Ozalay, the surrounding apartment blocks contained many families, whose children would play in the street below. Consequently, come bayram, a long stream of street gamines would be thumping our door.

"Bayram!" each would shout.

"Bayram! Bayram!" they would continue, raising their voices and thrusting out their palms.

"Bayram! Bayram!" and we would push a few coins into their hands so that they would clear off.

But not for long. There was an infantile grapevine at work passing the word along far and wide that at our apartment was a foreign couple who were ripe for the taking. So we were asked to fund far more children than we ever saw playing in the streets. I suspect that had they plied their trade at a Cypriot house, the result would not be a money gift but something more along the lines of, "Clear off, you little blighters!!"

The Institute had actually made an effort for Christmas this year. Unlike the previous year, there were Christmas trees here and there and the Institute was officially closed. On Christmas Day, Loydz attended the mass at the Saint Elizabeth Catholic Church and read the lesson as she did every Sunday, after which the impressive, avuncular Vice-Chancellor Rick had organised a Christmas get-together for some of the internationals. It was a thoughtful gesture to acknowledge that for many expatriates, Christmas Day can be the most homesick day of all. He invited some of the multilingual guests to offer Chrsitmas toasts in their mother tongues—from Welsh to German to Hindi. Loydz offered Christmas best wishes in her native Tagalog.

The Boxing Day event was not nearly so jolly. It was a dinner organised by Cemaliye at a hotel, the Aurora, which we had never before heard of. After my evening class we booked Adnam to take us there. The evening started badly when we realised that Adnam was in one of his manic moods.

He picked us up from the Institute just after eight o'clock, his "Five minutes, OK?" being just about right for once. As he hit the short stretch of motorway which skirts the town it became obvious that he was in one of his fast-driving phases when nothing under seventy miles per hour over any sort of terrain would be considered. At other times he would take the same mile of road at a tedious fifteen mph but tonight he was literally on song, driving along a darkened country road like a stock car racer, all the while muttering and singing to himself. Naturally he overshot the turning and we found ourselves driving in the Mercedes at high speed across a building site. Adnam was nonplussed.

"No problem! No problem!" as he slammed on the brakes and did a 180-degree hand-brake turn.

"OK! No problem! OK", which he kept repeating between tuneless singing and incomprehensible muttering.

We returned to the feeder road and made an abrupt right turn down the hill into the town. Adnam had resumed his speed and must have recovered some mental alertness because he was able to stamp all his weight on the brakes as soon as we were on top of the main town roundabout where the main road to Nicosia intersects the east-west traffic artery, a junction in particularly heavy use at eight-thirty on a holiday Friday evening. Soon we were off again up the hill to the Aurora Hotel where tonight's festivities were to be held. Adnam could not be contained.

"Adnam, slow down!" we implored, which only caused him to jump on the brakes and try to stop in the middle of the highway.

"OK! OK! No problem! One minute!" was all he could say, plus of course the random muttering, before switching all his weight to the accelerator pedal and lurching forward into the night.

We escaped Adnam's lunatic driving when he dumped us at the Aurora Hotel where the tables for the party were laid out in a large square, like one of those layouts they use for important international peace conferences between four governments. We found places next to the rest of the MIS team and went to help ourselves to the buffet. The food, which had been waiting for an hour, was cold. The music was not available and it was only with difficulty that I found a waiter to bring me wine. Amazingly, I also later got a second glass which must be some kind of record in this alcohol-phobic land. Apart from the cold food and a squirmingly embarrassing exchange of anonymous gifts between faculty members, the proceedings were mostly low-key and after half an hour we were planning our escape.

It occurred to me then as it often does in Northen Cyprus, how different it would be if the Turkish Cypriot people, like so many happier Mediterraneans do, were to drink alcohol as a lubricant of conviviality. The country is so-called 'liberal' Muslim and alcohol is not prohibited. Indeed Northern Cyprus even produces some goodish local wines. But in public at least, the Turkish Cypriot will not be seen partaking of nature's liquid sunshine. I wonder how many social occasions are ruined because they never reach the take-off point which marks to line between success and disaster, when a few shared glasses of wine would land it on the success side of that fine divide.

Instead, the local vice is tobacco, a dismal, solitary, selfish pleasure. But one which is not religiously proscribed. It was very depressing to see even young teenagers smoking. Most of the students smoked and it was very unpleasant to have to endure their smells when they crowded into my room. Even non-smoking students picked up the smells on their clothes and complained. At a party there is something unnatural about the sombre atmosphere which follows from rationing wine and other drinks while letting the smokers pollute the air.

Old attitudes die hard. When I see what could have been a friendly enjoyable social evening dropped flat on its face because no one would dare be seen drinking, I wondered if all Turkish parties are like this—a low-key, glum attempt to generate a friendly atmosphere while everyone is counting the minutes until it is polite to go home.

We English party easily because we have no inhibitions about the demon drink, a trait we share with most of our fellow Europeans. As a Cypriot taxi driver said to me censoriously when we he was driving us back from a Sunday lunch which had included a couple of glasses,

"All English drink. All the time. Drink all the time. Ver' bad. Ver' bad."

I took in, for a moment, the stale tobacco stink of his car before I replied.

"All Turkish smoke. All the time. Smoke all the time. Very bad. Very bad.

Fifteen

Before we could get on a plane to Sofia, I still had one more set of exams to oversee, although, to my relief, I would be away before I would have to face another assault on my sanity when the next registration came around. Having lived through five rounds of midterm or final exams by now, I was primed for what to expect. This, my final brush with the system, lived up to expectations with its usual farrago of cheating, collusion, fake ID's, 'ghost' students and all the rest of the panoply of student dishonesty and deviousness which any teacher at the Institute must grow to love or go mad. Unless that is he takes it seriously and tries to correct it, of course. Such reformers do not last long at the AIC—if they are not fired for upsetting the natural rhythm of the business machine, they will run a strong risk of the diseases of frustration such as apoplexy and mental instability. Far easier, I figured, to go with the flow and keep my sanity.'What can't be cured must be endured' as my old mother used to say. As an experiment to find out what they would say, I did tell one of my classes the story, reported in *The Guardian* some time in the 1970's, of an Indian university where final exams were supervised by the local students union. The story goes that they rigged up a PA system over which the examination answers were read out at dictation speed. Most of my class thought that that was a very good idea indeed.

Much to my interest, the student preparation for my last encounter with the Kyrenian exam circus introduced a new variation on the old theme of taking lecture notes into the exam on very thin paper folded up into a postage stamp size. Possibly because of the prohibition on using commercial external photocopying shops, students had learned that the faculty photocopier was not, unlike the photocopier factory at the campus book store, in continuous use. The faculty photocopier was, in fact, under the very strict control of Cemaliye, the faculty secretary, whose job it was carefully to ration small quantities of copy paper to teachers who needed to use it. As a result, most teachers would avoid the indignity of requesting half a dozen sheets of paper to print off essential classroom materials. So, when it was not actually broken, the faculty photocopier was idle for extended periods. This had not gone unnoticed by our cunning, quick-witted students who then used this slack time for mass-producing multiple copies of lecture notes for all those students who would not have been able to actually attend the class but were going to be taking the final exam. The small room housing the copier was kept locked, of course, precisely to stop the students doing just that. So how did the students get the key? Stupid question. This is Cyprus.

In my final week at Kyrenia, I was very busy. Reban would be taking over as head of department, something which he did not particularly want, especially since he would be required to teach at the MBA level. But since the Institute had been quite happy to let TFC teach MIS at all levels, without her knowing very much about any branch of information systems or computer technology, then Reban would come across as a high-powered geek by comparison. Add to the mix a few part-timers recruited off the street and a complete team for teaching the entire subject would be in place, at least for a term—everything from the basics, such as switching on the computer, right up to PhD courses in distributed databases and artificial intelligence could be left in safe hands.

So I made sure that my desk would be left completely clear for the handover. There were several days wall-to-wall grading—four courses, about two hundred final exam scripts and term papers and a panel of MBA dissertation oral examinations which I had to chair.

Again, the haphazard organisation of the Institute managed to turn the simple administrative procedure of a graduate *viva voce* into a stressful paperchase. First, the Head of the Graduate School would not accept my hand-typed report of the proceedings with the accompanying signatures of my co-panellists. No, he said, there is a special form which you must download from the Institute intranet. Which I did—three copies to be signed by the panel members. This involved me contacting the other two again before they disappeared for term break. Then I had to get the form signed by the Dean of Business. After a day or two he sent the form back with the message that the form was wrong and would I please get everything re-done on the new form please? So another trek to find my fellow panel members, who were now only showing up at the for their exam invigilations. Meanwhile I was being assailed daily by the three Iranian MBA candidates who were anxious to get the whole business straightened out so that they could buy their air tickets and leave the island prison for ever. Entirely reasonably, they did not trust the Institute to complete the process of awarding their diplomas in their absence so they were forced to stay in Cyprus and spend long hours monitoring my actions move by move so that no bureaucratic requirement could be left undone which would be an excuse for the Institute to withhold their degrees and demand yet another fee. A simple clerical operation, which, in a well-ordered organisation could be attended to by one person in say, an hour, was therefore transformed, under the malicious magic of the AIC, into a two-day nightmare. Kafka would have been seriously impressed.

In addition to my grading I also had to perform my share of invigilations, both of my own classes and those of my colleagues in business, politics and economics. Naturally, being a foreigner and moreover, a foreigner who was demob-happy at the prospect of escape, the faculty secretary was kind enough to award me considerably more classes to invigilate than would have been my normal share. But then it was the well-connected faculty secretary who held the real power: the heads of department were, in effect, little more than her clerical support staff. My administrative duties as head consisted almost entirely of work that should have been done by clerks or secretaries. That and being available for a continuous stream of students who would barge into my office at five-minute intervals with trivial problems about which they would whinge to me in halting broken English and draw out the incident to the limit of its mind-screaming fatuousness.

"Plis, professor, I wan' pliss. My staj. You take?"

See how concise is the Turkish language? 'Staj" translates into English as 'Summer Internship Formal Residency Report".

"You mean your summer internship report due in five months ago?"

"Plis professor, my staj!"

"You want me to take it now?"

"Plis, professor, my staj!"

"OK, I will take it."

"Plis professor. You take my staj?"

"Yes, just give it to me."

"But, professor, you no und'stan'. My staj. She is late."

"I know, just hand it over."

"But professor, my grade. Late my staj becos no feeneesh write when come Cyprus.

I have good grade for me? I work very very."

"Just leave it there, on the desk."

"I leave here, professor. You take now?"

"Just put it down on the desk."

"I leave it here, pliss, professor."

"Thank you. I will grade it."

"You grade? I get good grade? Work very, very! My friend he wait now also."

"Send him in."

Then there would be two or more of them in the office. Like comedy hour at the lunatic asylum they would keep up a multipart counterpoint of high-volume semi-comprehensible patter until I could feel my grip on my sanity starting to ebb away. After they had left I would usually need to take two or three minutes to suppress my suicidal impulses before there would be another knock on the office door and its accompanying thumps as the student attempted to open it.

"Plis professor, I have question. My staj. I give you. You grade it now already?"

I always kept my door locked even though it would mean I would need to get up to open it at least forty times a day for the reason that if I left it unlocked, as some faculty did, the students would be in my office seven or eight at a time from early morning until close of business which would deny me even those few moments of sanity and lucidity between morale-sapping ten-minute encounters necessary to negotiate the handing-in of a term paper or to confirm the date of an exam.

But now I was leaving and soon the style and honour of being 'Professor Doctor Head of Department' would be a mere unhappy distant memory.

So as not to leave Reban with any problems I made sure that all my grades were turned in to various places and in both electronic and paper copies (triplicated in both media) and my office was stripped bare of anything which might connect me with it.

Only one problem remained, the laptop. I spent a couple of hours removing all my personal files from it. I know they would be recoverable by a dedicated computer recovery expert but I was fairly sure that the AIC IT department would not be able to do that given their famous record for competence and efficiency. So I cleaned it up as best I could and phoned IT.

"My laptop. You can pick it up from my office at any time."

"Mehraba! What you want?"

"My laptop. You can get it now. Or, if you like, I can pass it on to someone who hasn't got one."

"What you mean? You feeneeshed laptop? Laptop kaput?"

"I am leaving. You can have your laptop back."

"Momen". I geeve you boss."

"Sir! Good morning!"

"I do not need my laptop now so you can pick it up. Or, if you like I can pass it on to Mr. Khan, who hasn't got one."

"No Professor Payne, that is not possible. You must bring it here to my office so that I can sign it out."

"No, I think I will leave it in my office so that you can collect it."

"That is not possible. You must bring it to me."

I dug my heals in, mindful that IT has keys to all the offices and had actually broken into my office on one occasion and taken a good look at my own machine after they had taken back the machine on the pretence of doing some software refit.

"No, that is not possible. I will not bring it to you. I am a senior professor and you are junior support staff. I am not trekking across campus in the pouring rain when one of you underemployed people can come to collect it."

"Professor Payne. I am telling you that you must bring it here. You are a member of the Institute and you must follow the rules and turn in the computer so that I can sign it off."

"No, I am not a member of the Institute anymore. If you want your computer you must come for it here."

"Professor Payne, if you do not bring the computer here, we will not pay you."

Could he do this, I wondered? Maybe he could. Like many incompetents at the Institute, he held his job via cronyism and by being a member of the ruling inner circle. Maybe he could persuade the payroll office not to pay me my well-earned January money. We would see. But this was no time to back down.

"Well. I am not bringing it so that's the end of the matter. If you don't like it, you can always sue me in the French courts."

A Pyrrhic victory? Possibly, but sometimes it is sweet to slam down the phone. Whatever the price.

So, all grades turned in after another reconciliation struggle at the office of the registrar between the names on my lists and the names on their lists and after hearing the news that the faculty pay-cut had been confirmed and that, to save money, students would need to pay tuition for a whole year, and not a term at a time. After carefully wiping clean the laptop, and after removing every trace of my occupancy of my office, I was ready to leave. The tickets from Cyprus to Sofia were bought and we dedicated the last Friday of the Kyrenian winter term to travelling.

Only one obstacle remained, the dreaded trip to the hell which is Istanbul Airport. Many have said that 'Heathrow' and 'Airport' are the two ugliest words in the English language. A wild claim like that could only be made by someone who has never been to Istanbul. So when we got there, with full immigration documentation, we paid over the transit visa scam extortion money and then found that they had changed the system. Europeans could, henceforth, proceed through passport control to pick up their luggage. Non-Europeans, even those whose papers were in order, would need to join a scrum of maybe two hundred people forming a shouting crowd in front of a desk where two Turkish clerks without a word of English were scrutinizing passports. Every few minutes someone escaped from this melee and was sent up stairs to check in. Their bags were, of course, outside in the customs area which they were not allowed access to. As far as we could see, it was completely impossible to be processed by immigration and retrieve one's luggage. Which is probably why there were so many people shouting at the two clerks in every English accent under the sun.

Unlike most of the poor people in this shouting horde, I could actually get our cases because my passport would let me reach the carousel. But Loydz was to be processed in the Tower of Babel and she would be there for some time. After retrieving our suitcases, I found that I was not allowed into the departure lounge because our flight out was not due for a few hours yet. But somehow, by bluff, bluster and the offering of money I managed to find the departure lounge to look for my wife. I tried to use my cellphone but its coverage did not extend to mainland Turkey. I tried to buy a new SIM card but the man selling phone cards did not have any. Finally I put a message out over the loudspeaker via the information desk. Thus, after about two hours of struggle and misery we had completed the first stage of our struggle against the Brueghelian horrors of the Istanbul Airport system. Next stop, Sofia.